A History of Just About Everything

Everything

180 Events, People and Inventions That Changed the World

Written by Elizabeth MacLeod
and Frieda Wishinsky

Illustrated by Qin Leng

Kids Can Press

Contents

A walk through history 5

ca 6 000 000 BCE First humans appear 6

ca 400 000 BCE Fire discovered........................ 7

ca 50 000 BCE Language developed 8

ca 40 000 BCE First cave paintings 8

ca 8000 BCE Humans begin farming................. 9

ca 8000 BCE Last big Ice Age ends 10

ca 7000 BCE First cities appear 10

ca 3500 BCE Horses first ridden........................ 11

ca 3500 BCE Wheel invented 12

ca 3500 BCE Plow invented............................... 12

ca 3500 BCE Sail invented 13

ca 3200 BCE Water pump invented 13

ca 3200 BCE Written language developed 14

ca 2560 BCE Great Pyramid of Giza built........ 15

ca 2000 BCE Concept of zero developed 15

ca 2200 BCE Rise of Greece............................. 16

ca 1500 BCE Iron Age begins........................... 17

ca 1100 BCE Alphabet developed 17

776 BCE First Olympic Games 18

ca 753 BCE Founding of Rome 18

ca 560 BCE Buddha is born 19

ca 551 BCE Confucius is born 19

508 BCE First voting..20

ca 400 BCE Hippocrates revolutionizes
    medicine...20

ca 250 BCE Compass invented 21

ca 250 BCE Archimedes changes math
    and science 21

ca 221 BCE Great Wall of China built 22

ca 100 BCE Silk Road flourishes 23

ca 100 BCE Rise of the Roman Empire 24

ca 5 BCE Jesus Christ is born 25

79 Mount Vesuvius erupts 25

105 Cai Lun invents paper.......................26

ca 250 Golden age of the Maya 27

ca 500 Spinning wheel invented 28

ca 570 Muhammad is born 28

ca 800 Printing invented............................29

ca 800 ibn Hayyan develops scientific method ..29

ca 800 Age of the Vikings 30

1044 Gunpowder invented 32

1096 Crusades begin 32

1206 Genghis Khan rules Mongol Empire 33

1215 King John signs Magna Carta 34

1271 Marco Polo treks to China 35

ca 1277 Huygens invents mechanical clock 35

1286 Eyeglasses invented 36

1337 Hundred Years' War begins 36

ca 1347 Black Death breaks out....................36

ca 1400 Renaissance begins 37

ca 1440 Gutenberg invents printing press 38

ca 1490 Aztec Empire at peak.........................39

1492 Columbus reaches the Americas 40

1497 Cabot reaches the "New World" 40

1503 Da Vinci paints *Mona Lisa* 41

1508 Michelangelo paints Sistine Chapel
    ceiling...41

1510 African slaves first shipped to
    the Americas..42

1519 Magellan sets out to sail around
    the world 43

1519 Cortés meets the Aztecs 43

1520 Suleiman rules the Ottoman Empire........44

1526 Mughal Empire begins..........................44

1543 Copernicus shows Earth orbits the Sun ...45

ca 1595 Shakespeare writes *Romeo and Juliet* ...45

1600 Gilbert explains electricity
and magnetism 46

1607 Jamestown becomes first colony
in America..47

1608 Champlain establishes permanent
settlement in Canada 47

1609 Kepler publishes his laws of planetary
motion 48

1609 Galileo revolutionizes astronomy............48

1687 Newton "invents" physics 49

ca 1690 Dodo becomes extinct 49

1751 Discovery of the commercial potential
of rubber..49

1759 Defeat of the French in Canada...............50

1768 Cook explores the Pacific Ocean 50

1776 Steam engine invented 51

1776 American Revolution 52

1781 Industrial Revolution begins in England...53

1789 French Revolution 54

1790 Mozart composes.................................55

1796 Jenner develops vaccines......................55

1800 Volta invents electric battery 56

1809 Appert develops first canned food 56

1816 Laënnec invents stethoscope 56

1821 Faraday invents electric motor................57

1822 Babbage invents a computer...................57

1824 Braille invented 58

1825 Stephenson builds first steam railway 58

1826 Niépce takes first photographs................59

1842 Synthetic fertilizer invented..................59

1844 Morse demonstrates electric telegraph......60

1854 Nightingale revolutionizes nursing 61

1856 Bessemer makes steel cheaply.................61

1859 Darwin presents his theory of evolution....62

1859 Lenoir invents internal combustion
engine..63

ca 1862 Pasteur's experiments lead to
pasteurization 63

1866 Transatlantic telegraph cable links
continents 64

1866 Mendel experiments with genes 64

1869 Suez Canal completed...........................65

1876 Refrigerator invented...........................65

1876 Bell invents telephone..........................66

1878 Fleming establishes standard time zones ..67

1880 Edison invents lightbulb........................67

1885 Benz builds first car 68

1893 Women get the vote.............................68

1895 Röntgen discovers X-rays 69

1898 Curie discovers two new elements 69

1900 Television invented...............................70

1901 Marconi sends radio signal
across Atlantic 70

1903 Wright brothers fly first airplane 71

1904 Digging the Panama Canal......................72

1905 Einstein discovers $E=mc^2$ 72

1907 Baekeland invents plastic.......................73

1909 Peary reaches the North Pole 74

1911 Art goes abstract.................................74

1912 *Titanic* sinks 75

1913 Bohr explains the atom..........................75

1914 World War I 76

1917 Russian Revolution and rise of
communism 78

1917 Rutherford splits the atom 79
1918 Fatal flu kills millions 79
1920 Carver revolutionizes agriculture 80
1922 King Tut's tomb discovered 80
1922 Banting develops insulin 81
1927 Robot revolution begins 82
1928 Fleming develops penicillin 82
1929 Wall Street crashes 83
1930 Building the Empire State Building 83
1930 Gandhi's Salt March 84

1933 Hitler seizes power in Germany 85
1936 Berlin Olympics and the Nazis 85
1939 World War II 86
1939 First computer built 88
1939 Nuclear fission discovered 89
1945 Atomic bomb is dropped 89
1945 United Nations established 90
1947 Transistor invented 90
1948 Creation of the State of Israel 91
1949 People's Republic of China established 91
1953 DNA molecule unraveled 92
1953 Hillary and Norgay climb
    Mount Everest 92
1955 Salk develops polio vaccine 93
1957 First satellite launched 93
1958 Kilby invents microchip 94
1959 Leakey discovers ancient skull 94
1960 First woman prime minister 94
1960 Maiman invents laser 94
1961 Berlin Wall separates a city 95
ca 1962 Beatles revolutionize music 96
1962 Silent Spring warns of environmental
    danger 96
1963 King's "I have a dream" speech 97
1963 Kennedy assassinated 97
1969 Humans land on the Moon 98

1969 Internet developed 100
1971 Guillet invents biodegradable plastic 100
1973 Cooper invents cell phone 100
1975 Personal computer invented 101
1976 Viking spacecraft lands on Mars 102
1977 Star Wars revolutionizes moviemaking .. 102
1979 Iranian revolution 103
ca 1980 HIV/AIDS spreads 103
1986 Chernobyl nuclear reactor disaster 104
1989 Oil spill in Alaska 104
1989 Tiananmen Square protest 105
1989 Communism in Europe collapses 105
1990 Mandela is freed 106
1990 Hubble Space Telescope launched 106
1991 World Wide Web takes off 107
1993 MP3s make music 107
1993 European Union comes together 108
1994 Chunnel rail tunnel opens 108
1996 First mammal cloned 109

1997 First Harry Potter book 109
2001 Terrorists attack World Trade Center
    and Pentagon 110
2003 Social networking takes off 110
2003 Space Shuttle Columbia explodes 111
2003 Heat wave in Europe 111
2008 Search for life on Mars 112
2008 Obama becomes president of the
    United States 113
2010 Floods, earthquakes and more
    natural disasters 113
2010 Icelandic volcano disrupts travel 113
2010 Oil spill in Gulf of Mexico 114
2010 The Arab revolutions 114
2011 Japanese earthquake 115
20?? What's the next big deal? 115
Time line 116
Index 121

A walk through history

There are moments no one forgets: a boy in the early 1900s sees the first car drive down his street; a family in the 1920s buys its first radio; a soldier hears that World War II is over; a mother and her daughter look up on September 11, 2001, and see a plane crash into the World Trade Center.

The inventions and events that created those moments changed the lives of individuals and countries in ways big and small, and often for years afterward.

Learning about history makes you realize that what happens in one place and time can spill over to another. Each event creates a ripple effect. Sometimes we don't know what the ripple will be till years later.

In this book, we take you on a walk through history. We've chosen events we thought were important and explained how they rippled forward to affect the future.

History, of course, is more than just dates and facts. It's also about how people interpret what happened. Especially for long-ago events, there are often many interpretations. Sometimes finding new artifacts or discovering new dating techniques can change earlier interpretations. But one thing is certain. What happened yesterday, last year, 100 years ago, or even 100 000 years ago affects our lives today.

In these pages, we hope to show how we are all part of, and linked to, the past, the present and the future. In the body of the text or in special "Ripples" boxes, we show how each event rippled forward to change the world.

A note about dates

Dates for some events, especially those from ancient times (such as the date of the beginning of agriculture), are often difficult to pin down. If a precise date is not known, we've used the abbreviation "ca," which stands for the Latin *circa*, meaning "around." So "ca 6000" means "around the year 6000." We've also used BCE, which is short for "before the common era," to refer to dates before the year 1. BCE is used instead of BC ("before Christ") because it is acceptable to all peoples.

ca 400 000 BCE: Fire is discovered.

ca 2560 BCE: The Great Pyramid of Giza is built.

1876: Bell invents the telephone.

1903: The Wright brothers take flight.

1969: Humans land on the Moon.

ca 6 000 000 BCE **First humans appear**

About six million years ago, *Sahelanthropus*, one of our earliest human ancestors, may have swung down from a tree in Africa and started to walk upright. He had a smaller brain than we do, a flatter face and a heavy eyebrow ridge. In fact, he looked a bit like an ape, which is not surprising — humans descended from apes more than six million years ago.

Walking on two legs gave early humans lots of advantages over other animals. Standing upright made them taller, so they could see farther to look for food or spot danger. Having their arms free allowed them to carry things, use tools or fight.

As humans' brains developed and grew bigger, our ancestors wanted to explore and see what was beyond the next hill. About 1.8 million years ago, some early humans began to leave Africa. They first traveled to Eurasia (now China and India). Later, about 800 000 years ago, humans arrived in Europe.

About 200 000 years ago, *Homo sapiens* — modern humans like us — evolved in Africa. They migrated to the Middle East around 125 000 years ago, then on to South Asia by 50 000 years ago. They also sailed to Australia around that time. About 40 000 years ago, *Homo sapiens* arrived in Europe, and in East Asia approximately 10 000 years after that.

No one knows for sure when humans traveled to North America. Sometime between 30 000 and 14 000 years ago, they likely sailed from Asia across the North Pacific. Then they continued down the west coast of North America and even as far south as South America.

RIPPLES

As you turn the pages of this book, you'll discover the many ways humans have changed the world. Controlling fire (see page 7) was one of humans' first big achievements — it led to changes in diet, society, even body hair!

Humans, it turned out, were good problem solvers and went on to invent everything from the wheel (page 12) to the printing press (page 38) to the World Wide Web (page 107). We've also always been curious, exploring new lands, new ideas and new ways of doing things. For instance, Nicolaus Copernicus revolutionized people's ideas about the universe (page 45),

New Zealand women toppled the men-only club of politics when they got the vote (page 68), and Facebook (page 110) changed how people keep in touch.

Not all the events in human history have been positive. Wars, especially World War II (page 86), have ravaged countries, and the hunger for more resources has put a strain on the planet. The future poses new problems to solve, such as fuel, food and water shortages and climate change. Maybe your ideas will help solve some of the world's problems and put you in the history books, too!

ca 400 000 BCE Fire discovered

Maybe lightning zapped a tree and set it on fire. Or perhaps an early human rubbed two rocks together, sending a spark flying and starting some grass burning. No one knows exactly when or how people discovered fire or learned to control it, but it was a huge advance in human civilization.

With the warmth of the fire, humans could move to colder climates. But they also no longer needed their heavy body hair and gradually lost it. Without so much hair, they could hunt in the hot part of the day when most furry animals are snoozing and easier to catch.

Fire also meant people had light, so they could stay up later, which gave them more time to make tools and bond with each other. And fire protected them from insects and wild animals.

People began to sleep huddled around a fire with others. That meant they had to develop tolerance of others and build relationships.

About 400 000 years ago, someone dropped some meat in a fire, either by accident or on purpose. When she pulled it out and popped it in her mouth — yum! Gradually, people's digestive tracts shrank because cooked food was easier to process than tough, raw food. Softer food also led to smaller teeth. Brains got bigger, and with better nutrition people got bigger, too, and began living longer.

RIPPLES

People began to use fire in new ways. They used the smoke to send messages. Artists drew with charred sticks. Some of their artwork still survives in caves (page 8). By 29 000 years ago, people were putting pottery in bonfires to "fire" it to make it stronger.

About 8000 years ago, farmers began burning fields to remove grasses so they could plant crops. As early as 5500 years ago, people in the Middle East used fire to melt bronze and make such things as tools, decorations and weapons.

When people boiled water over fire, they got more than just tea — they made steam. Many years later, in 1776, that became the power for a new kind of engine (page 51). Talk about setting the world on fire!

ca 50 000 BCE Language developed

All animals communicate. Whales sing to one another, birds chirp and bees dance to show where the best flowers are. But only humans have developed a system, called language, that lets people communicate with each other about everything from videos of kittens to tonight's homework to world peace.

In the beginning, people communicated with gestures. But if their hands were busy with tools or they couldn't see each other, hand signals didn't work. So about 50 000 years ago, humans began making sounds to communicate. At first, these were probably only grunts and hoots, but as humans evolved, so did the sounds they could make.

Unlike other animals, humans have complex vocal cords. They allow us to make more sounds than other animals and more complex sounds. Many animals have a throat, tongue and lips, but these parts in humans are more flexible, and we're able to control them better.

Long ago, humans learned to match a sound to an object. So the sounds *ap* and *hull*, for instance, were linked to an apple. Soon verbs, adjectives and even grammar were created to make language more useful and easier to understand.

ca 40 000 BCE First cave paintings

Scientists and archaeologists now believe that the first cave paintings were made by Stone Age artists about 40 000 years ago. The paintings of red dots, disks, lines and hands were created in northwestern Spain. They appeared about 10 000 years before the lifelike drawings of animals like the ones you see here, from Chauvet, France.

With each new cave art discovery, there is renewed debate about why ancient people painted images. Was it for religious, ceremonial or purely artistic purposes? Were they trying to record what they saw or hunted? The meaning of cave paintings and their sites continues to be analyzed and discussed.

ca 8000 BCE Humans begin farming

For thousands of years, people fed themselves by hunting animals and gathering plants, nuts and berries. When these hunter-gatherers had eaten all the food in one area, they gathered their belongings and moved to a new area.

Hunting was dangerous and difficult, so people came up with a better idea. Around 8000 BCE, farmers in Africa and the areas around Iraq, Turkey and Israel likely began keeping wild sheep in caves. Gradually the sheep became domesticated. People began penning in other animals, including wild pigs and cows. Soon herding, not hunting, became a way of life in many areas of the world.

Around 6000 BCE, farmers in the Middle East developed wheat, rye, barley and other crops by breeding local wild grains. Rice was developed from a wild grass people domesticated along the Chang River in China. Today, some crops, including rice, have to be cultivated by humans — they no longer grow in the wild.

RIPPLES

Growing crops and raising animals changed food production. An area that once had provided enough food for only about 10 hunter-gatherers could feed 1000 people through farming. That meant populations could grow — and fast.

Since people no longer had to move around to find food, they didn't have to worry about only having belongings they could carry. They began to build permanent homes and other buildings and acquire possessions. Most of these communities were near rivers and lakes so farmers could water their crops.

Farmers kept trying to improve production. That led to such inventions as the plow (page 12) and synthetic fertilizer (page 59).

For almost 10 000 years, civilizations were built on agriculture and farm labour. It wasn't until the Industrial Revolution (page 53) began in the 1700s that farming started to give way to a new way of making a living — manufacturing.

Today, about one-third of the world's workers have jobs in farming. Agriculture provides much more than just food and clothing. We depend on it for fuels (ethanol and biodiesel, for example), bioplastics (plastics made from plants rather than oil) and medicines.

ca 8000 BCE Last big Ice Age ends

The Earth was cold. From about 100 000 BCE on, huge, thick sheets of ice covered most of the northern hemisphere. They formed as Earth's climate cooled over thousands of years.

Then about 10 000 years ago, the climate began to grow warmer, and the ice sheets started to melt. By about 8000 BCE, the last ice sheets had retreated in northern Europe and northern North America. People began to move into areas that had previously been icebound. They fanned out across Europe and North America, establishing small communities in these areas for the first time.

ca 7000 BCE First cities appear

It was around 7000 BCE that people likely founded the city of Jericho, located in the Middle East. Today, it's the world's oldest continuously lived-in city. Jericho is near the Jordan River, and there are many water springs in and around the city. Having water close by was important to early people for drinking, washing and watering crops that grew in the fields around the city.

How did cities first come about? After people stopped moving around hunting and gathering their food, they began to farm (page 9). The development of agriculture made it possible for a field to support more people. The population grew, and people began to live closer together.

Soon early farmers began to trade. A farmer who had an extra sheep might trade it for grain. As more and more people traded, they started to gather in certain places that eventually became markets. Towns grew up around these markets.

People found there were lots of advantages to living together in towns. They didn't have to travel far to trade with each other. Neighbors were close enough to help each other and fight off invaders or thieves. When a settlement grew big enough, new businesses could develop, such as basket making and pottery.

Workers from different backgrounds were brought together in towns and cities. People could exchange ideas easily, which generated new ideas. People saw that working with others allowed them to accomplish more. Together they formed a society. Life became easier. New societies formed, depending on what people were achieving, their culture and what they had to trade.

Of course, there were problems, too, so cities learned to deal with crime, diseases, pollution and other issues. Governments formed to look after these things.

Today's cities are big and bustling. The largest ones, such as Karachi in Pakistan, China's Shanghai and India's Mumbai, are each home to more than 15 million people.

ca 3500 BCE Horses first ridden

Imagine riding a pig. What about a cow? Pigs, cows, sheep — even cats — were domesticated long before horses. But horses are still one of few animals that people ride. Horses likely changed history more than any other animal because they carried explorers to new territories and soldiers into battle.

As long as 15 000 years ago, people in Europe hunted wild horses for meat. Then they began herding them like sheep and milking them. These people were nomads, which means they moved around a lot. At one point they used dogs to carry their belongings. But the nomads soon discovered that horses could carry heavier packs than dogs or pull bundles on sleds.

About 6500 years ago, someone may have scrambled onto the back of a horse to adjust a pack. Or maybe someone climbed up on a horse to see farther. Experts say it was on the Eurasian Steppe (plains that stretch from Hungary to Mongolia) that people first discovered the advantages of horseback riding.

Horses helped people move faster than ever before. They made hunting and herding easier, too. Horses also sped up message delivery, which improved communications.

As early as 4000 BCE, soldiers began riding horses into war. Around 800 BCE, the first saddle was created to make riding easier. Stirrups, first used about 200 BCE, allowed a rider to control the horse while the horseman was fighting.

But slower-moving farm workhorses changed the world, too. Out in the fields, they pulled plows, wagons and other farm machinery. Horses also carried heavy loads of wheat or vegetables long distances. That allowed farmers to take their goods to villages, which made the farmers richer. It also brought those tiny towns into contact with larger cities. Horses also carried lumber and stone into cities, which meant more supplies were available to shipbuilders, carpenters and other builders.

RIPPLES

Although machines and trucks have mostly replaced horses, the word "horsepower" is still used to measure a vehicle's power. And there are jobs that horses do better than any machine. Cowboys on horseback round up cattle over rugged terrain that would destroy any vehicle. In other rough areas, horses are used to search for lost people or to clear trails. And police rely on horses for keeping order in large crowds.

Now, most people just ride horses for fun, or watch them perform at races or in horse shows. There are about 60 million horses in the world today. They may be a little old-fashioned, but horses are definitely here to stay.

ca 3500 BCE Wheel invented

The first wheel likely didn't help people get around — it was probably a potter's wheel. Beginning around 3500 BCE, it helped people make jugs, bowls and other pottery more easily and faster than by hand.

Then around 3200 BCE, the Sumerians in ancient Mesopotamia (today's southern Iraq) began using wheels to move heavy loads. They attached the wheels to an axle (central shaft), and the wheels and axle turned together. It worked well, but if the chariot went around a corner too fast — CRASH!

The next step was probably to attach the axle to the vehicle and have the wheels spin around this fixed axle. Much better on turns.

The first cart wheels weren't like today's wheels — they were heavy, wooden slabs — until someone cut holes in them, creating spokes. Chariot wheels got spokes around 1600 BCE.

RIPPLES

Wheels allowed people to move heavy loads. Food and supplies could be transported farther. But wheels roll better on smooth roads, so eventually paved roads were built. The roads linked communities so that people could trade goods and grow wealthier.

Today, most of our vehicles still depend on wheels, but so do lots of other machines, including clocks, computers and motors. The propeller, gyroscope and turbine have all developed from the wheel.

ca 3500 BCE Plow invented

Planting crops is hard work. Long ago in ancient Mesopotamia (today's southern Iraq), Sumerian farmers dragged a stick through the soil to make a trough into which they dropped seeds. When a blade was added to the stick, the plow was born.

The plow's blade cut into the soil and turned it over, bringing up nutrients and burying weeds. It also mixed air into the soil.

The plow made planting easier. And plowing itself got a lot easier when people hitched oxen, and later horses, to the plow. Soon people were growing more food than their families could eat. They could trade extra food for things they didn't have.

Farmers eventually covered the wooden blade with iron, making the plow even more efficient. Plows became steam powered around 1850 and later gasoline powered.

The plow allowed people to turn forests and grasslands into fields. By the 1930s, plows had cut through the grasses that had once held down the soil on North America's prairies. The soil blew away, and crop production plummeted. Thousands of people were forced off their farms in the "Dust Bowl."

Farmers still depend on the plow. Today, plows are also used underwater to lay cables and dig for oil.

ca 3500 BCE Sail invented

Egyptians were likely the first to attach sails to their boats. But how they came up with the idea lies buried in the past. Maybe an Egyptian trader was standing on a boat, shaking out a large piece of canvas or other cloth. Suddenly, wind caught the fabric, and the boat zoomed down the river.

The sail let people fish new areas and move cargoes by water. Later, sailors traveled to new lands and learned about their cultures.

The first sails were square. They were soon replaced by triangular sails. Over time, masts and rigging changed, too. So did knowledge of winds, currents and navigation. When the compass was invented (page 21), explorers could sail out of sight of land and return safely. During the Age of Discovery, from the early 1400s to the early 1600s, Europeans traveled the world on sailing ships, looking for new trade routes and new lands.

One problem with sailing ships was that they needed wind to move. When steamships were invented in the late 1700s, sailing ships were left in the lurch. Now they are used for sport and recreation, but long ago they changed the world.

ca 3200 BCE Water pump invented

The plow (page 12) made it easier to plant crops, but plants need water to grow. When there wasn't enough rain, what was a farmer to do?

Farmers in Mesopotamia (today's southern Iraq) carried water from the nearest river or lake. The first water pump was a pole with a leather bucket on one end. The farmer pushed down on the pole so that the bucket dropped into the water and filled. When the farmer let go, the weight at the other end helped lift the bucket. The bucket was then carried to the field or poured into a ditch to water, or irrigate, the crops.

This water pump, called a *shaduf*, was used in the Middle East for about 2000 years. Next came the *noria*, a pump that looked like a wheel with buckets around its rim. As the wheel turned, the buckets dipped into the water, which was then poured into an irrigation ditch.

The Archimedes' screw pump was developed around 250 BCE. It looked like a giant screw in a hollow tube. One end was placed in water so that when the screw turned, it drew water up the tube and out the other end. Well-watered land could feed more people. People could move closer together, so communities developed.

ca 3200 BCE Written language developed

The Sumerians' invention of writing changed their lives and ours. The Sumerians lived in Mesopotamia (today's southern Iraq). They established cities, farmed, herded animals, hunted, fished and traded. As their trading increased, they realized they needed a way to keep records. That's where writing comes in. To keep track of their business dealings, the Sumerians used simple pictograms. Each pictogram represented an object or an idea. So, for example, the pictogram for a hand looked like a simplified drawing of a hand.

The Sumerians used a reed stylus (stick) to carve the pictograms into wet clay tablets. When the clay hardened, the writing became a permanent record. Eventually, the Sumerians realized that drawing pictograms was too slow and cumbersome. So they further simplified their pictograms into wedge-shaped abstract symbols. We call this kind of writing cuneiform.

Now that they could communicate information in writing, the Sumerians set up schools for the wealthy, to pass on knowledge to the next generation. Writing also led to written laws, stories and poems. The most famous Sumerian story is called "The Epic of Gilgamesh," which describes the adventures of a king.

The Sumerians also invented other useful things, such as the plow and the wheel (page 12) and a system of mathematics based on the number 60. They were a practical, adaptable and clever people.

Unfortunately, although we can read Sumerian texts, understand their ideas and know much about their way of life, we have no record of how their language sounded.

RIPPLES

Even after the Sumerian civilization declined, writing survived and thrived.

As later people searched for easier ways to communicate, cuneiform led to the invention of the alphabet (page 17). People also looked for better materials than clay tablets on which to record information. The Egyptians began to make an early form of paper from papyrus, a plant that grows along the Nile River.

Today we have paper, pens, pencils — and keyboards — but we still use writing to share ideas and information.

ca 2560 BCE Great Pyramid of Giza built

It took more than 20 years to build the Great Pyramid of Giza in Egypt. When it was completed, it was the tallest human-made structure in the world. It held that record for more than 3800 years.

Its architects modeled its shape after a sacred pointed stone called the *benben*, which symbolized the rays of the Sun. Astronomers chose the site for the pyramid, and more than 20 000 laborers floated huge stones down the Nile River. Other workers cut and polished the stones to fit the structure. Thousands pushed the stones up ramps, and thousands more hauled them into position. Communities of bakers and cooks sprang up to feed the workers. It was an enormous, sweaty, exhausting project.

Why did the ancient Egyptians build it? The great pyramid was a tomb for King Khufu, but historians and archaeologists think it was even more than that. The ancient Egyptians believed that the pyramids would shield their country from harm and protect the pharaohs, their rulers, after death.

The Egyptians wrote many stories about what happens when a pharaoh dies. In one story he became the god Osiris, King of the Dead. A part of his spirit, his *ka*, stayed in his body and needed proper care so that he could carry out his new duties. And since the Egyptians believed that the pharaohs traveled to the heavens on a sunbeam, the pyramid, which is in the shape of a sunbeam, was a perfect place for the pharaoh to be buried.

RIPPLES

Building the Pyramid of Giza was a monumental undertaking. The pyramid has withstood wars, weather, thieves and time. It's one of the seven wonders of the ancient world and the last to survive. Its construction is still being studied, and it draws thousands of tourists a year to modern Egypt.

ca 2000 BCE Concept of zero developed

Zero might seem like — well, a big nothing. But imagine trying to do math without it. For instance, take the number 507. Mathematicians in ancient Babylon (where Iraq is today) simply left a space between the 5 and the 7. But that was confusing and inefficient. So around 2000 BCE, Babylonians created a mark to mean "nothing," or "absence."

Zero didn't always look like this: 0. The Babylonian zero looked a bit like this: YY. It was Chinese mathematicians who first used the oval that we now call zero.

The idea of zero as a real number seems obvious today. But thousands of years ago, it revolutionized mathematics.

ca 2200 BCE Rise of Greece

The Greek civilization, which became one of the most advanced of the ancient world, can be traced back more than 3500 years. Small communities formed near fertile farmland around the Aegean and Mediterranean Seas. Those communities developed and grew into the Greek civilization.

The Minoans, who lived on the Mediterranean island of Crete, established one of the first and most important of these settlements. By 2200 BCE the Minoans were thriving. They had good soil and grew grains, olives and grapes for wine. They became active traders and did business with nearby towns and places as far away as Egypt and Syria.

The Minoans built huge palaces with hundreds of rooms. One of these is Knossos on Crete, a site that archaeologists have studied extensively. It contains art that shows the Minoans were skilled artists, architects and engineers.

Eventually, the Minoan civilization was destroyed by a lethal combination of earthquakes, tsunamis and an invasion by the Mycenaeans from the nearby mainland.

The Mycenaeans became wealthy and powerful. They adapted Minoan art and architecture and were bold traders and excellent engineers and builders. Their culture reached its peak around 1600 BCE. Then gradually, over the next few centuries, the civilization declined, probably due to war or intense conflict between the rich and poor.

For a few centuries afterward, these towns fell into a dark age. The population dropped, and there was less trade and commerce.

By around 900 BCE, what we now call the Greek civilization started to emerge from this bleak period. As the population grew and prospered, the Greeks looked to surrounding lands for new sources of food and trade. They visited other parts of the Mediterranean and brought back new ideas.

From around 500 BCE on, Greek culture was at its height. The new ideas of great Greek thinkers, such as Socrates, Aristotle and Plato in philosophy, Hippocrates in medicine (page 20) and Pythagoras and Archimedes in mathematics and science (page 21) blossomed. The renowned Greek statesman Pericles advanced democratic ideals. The theories of all these men about art, mathematics, religion, medicine and democracy transformed the way people saw the world.

RIPPLES

During the early Middle Ages, Greek thinkers and their great ideas were almost forgotten. But during the Renaissance (page 37) in the 1400s, Greek ideas and books were rediscovered, discussed and appreciated again. That appreciation continues.

Greek ideas still influence modern society in art, philosophy, drama, mathematics, politics, education and medicine.

ca 1500 BCE Iron Age begins

Experts describe civilizations based on what they use for tools. For instance, the Stone Age lasted from about 2.6 million years ago to 4500 years ago (2500 BCE). That's when people used stone tools.

Next came the Bronze Age, when people learned how to make tools from this metal. It started at different times in various countries. This age lasted from about 3500 BCE to around 600 BCE in the Middle East.

The Iron Age began around 1500 BCE in Africa and Asia, and in Europe about 500 years later. Iron was probably discovered when someone dropped a rock into a fire, where it melted and then cooled into a strong metal.

Iron made farming tools more efficient, so that farmers could grow more food. No longer did people have to struggle to produce enough to eat. They had more time to do such things as make jewelry and other decorative objects.

Iron led to stronger weapons. And since there was lots of iron, there were lots of weapons — and wars. Countries started to have armies always standing by, ready to fight.

Some people say we're now in the Silicon Age because silicon is the material that makes computers (page 101) work. But we still use iron for farm machines, weapons and buildings.

ca 1100 BCE Alphabet developed

The Egyptians had an early form of alphabet, but it's the Phoenicians who get the credit for inventing an alphabet that was widely used and adapted.

The Phoenicians were sea traders who lived in what is now Lebanon, Syria and Israel. They traveled all over the Mediterranean to countries as far away as Tunisia, Spain, Portugal, Southern France and Sicily. With all that trade, the Phoenicians needed an easy system to record business deals. They found cuneiform writing slow, so they came up with a better system — an alphabet.

The Phoenician alphabet had 22 consonants but no vowels. It was written right to left, and their wordswererununtogetherlikethis. The Phoenicians eventually inserted dots between words — this•made•reading•easier.

Z	W	H	D	G	B	'
N	M	L	K	Y	T	H
T	SH	R	Q	S	P	'	S

776 BCE First Olympic Games

At the first recorded Olympic Games, in Olympus, Greece, a cook named Koroibos ran 192 m (210 yd.) naked and won the race, the only event of the Games. As time went on, the Games expanded to include more running events, as well as boxing, discus and javelin throwing, horse riding, jumping, wrestling and even chariot racing.

The Games were held every four years as a way for the Greeks to honor the king of their gods, Zeus.

At first, all male citizens could compete, except for criminals and slaves. Women and girls were mostly forbidden from taking part or even attending the Games. In time, athletes replaced ordinary citizens. There were strict rules forbidding athletes from accepting money for winning, and cheating was frowned upon. Winners received only an olive wreath, and their names were inscribed in the official record.

The Roman emperor Theodosius I, a Christian, didn't approve of the games glorifying pagan gods such as Zeus. He put an end to the Games in 391 CE.

RIPPLES

Some 1500 years later, Pierre de Coubertin of France revived the Olympics. The first modern Olympics took place in 1896 in Athens, Greece. The first Winter Olympics was held in 1924. Today, countries around the world vie to host the Olympic Games and cheer on their athletes.

ca 753 BCE Founding of Rome

According to legend, the city of Rome began with twins named Romulus and Remus. The boys were the sons of the war god Mars. They were abandoned at birth, nursed by a female wolf and raised by a shepherd. When the twins grew up, Romulus killed Remus and became the first king of Rome.

Archaeologists and historians don't know if any of this legend is based on fact. However, they do know that a city grew up on seven hills near the Tiber River in what is now Italy. The city was made up of small settlements of Latins, Sabines, Umbrians, Samnites and Etruscan peoples, who regularly fought each other. They also influenced each other's cultures and beliefs.

The Etruscan society, which was in turn influenced by Greek culture (page 16), had an especially big impact on Rome. The Etruscans were skilled engineers and artists. They mined iron, worked with metals and developed a calendar. The last king of Rome was an Etruscan called Tarquinius Superbus. In 509 BCE he was kicked out, and Rome became a republic, governed by the people rather than a king.

RIPPLES

The Roman Republic lasted till the beginning of the 1st century CE, when under the rule of emperors it grew into a vast and mighty empire (page 24).

ca 560 BCE Buddha is born

No one is sure exactly when Siddhartha Gautama, later known as the Buddha, was born.

According to legend, he was born in northern India to a family of local rulers. It's said that he left his rich family, shaved his head, put on beggar's robes and set off to find answers to questions about suffering, death and injustice.

One day, when he'd settled under a tree to meditate, he realized that enlightenment — a calm and untroubled state — could be achieved only by disciplining the mind. He believed that people's difficulties are a result of selfish desires, and that the way to escape pain and suffering is through compassion. It was around this time that he became known as the Buddha. (The word "Buddha" means "enlightened one.") He spent the rest of his life teaching and spreading his beliefs.

RIPPLES

Today Buddhism is practiced widely, mostly in Asia, and has about 376 million followers worldwide.

ca 551 BCE Confucius is born

"Forget injuries. Never forget kindness" is just one of the expressions attributed to Chinese philosopher Confucius.

Many details of his life are based on legends and were recorded long after his death. He was probably born to a warrior family in the Chinese state of Lu and brought up in poverty. He later married and had children. He held various jobs and rose to become a justice minister in Lu.

But he was not satisfied and left his job. He gathered disciples and taught his philosophy. He believed that people are responsible for their own actions. He felt that people should show compassion and not be boastful. He valued family and respect for elders.

Confucius has influenced many philosophers, and even today people try to live by his ideas, especially in China.

508 BCE First voting

People have probably voted for thousands of years. Every time they put up their hands to show support for an idea, they cast their vote.

But the first definite record of voting dates back to Greece in 508 BCE. The Greeks weren't picking their leaders — they were voting on which politicians to banish!

Voting is a way for people to have a say in their government and their future. Since each vote is worth as much as another, having a vote made people more equal. So a peasant became as important as the lord he toiled for.

ca 400 BCE Hippocrates revolutionizes medicine

Modern doctors owe a lot to Hippocrates. But although he revolutionized medicine, little is known about him. It is thought that he was born on the Greek island of Kos (or Cos) around 460 BCE and was probably trained in medicine by his father, who was also a physician.

Hippocrates' medical ideas contradicted many of the beliefs of his time. As a result, he was sent to prison for 20 years. There he wrote his theories about medicine.

What were his radical ideas? Back then, most people went to priests for medical advice. Hippocrates believed that priests should deal with spiritual matters — what you can't see. Medicine, he thought, is about what you *can* see. He also believed that illness was not a punishment of the gods, as the priests taught, but had natural causes.

Hippocrates didn't know all that much about anatomy, since dissecting dead bodies was taboo. Nevertheless, he felt it was important to observe patients closely. He insisted on good record keeping, so that a doctor could see if a patient was getting better or worse.

Hippocrates was careful to avoid using medicines or techniques that might be harmful to the patient.

Instead, he favored cleanliness, diet, sleep and soothing balms. He thought doctors should be professional, disciplined and attentive to the patient's progress and needs.

RIPPLES

Hippocrates and his followers changed medicine by carefully describing diseases and medical conditions. They noted symptoms and made diagnoses based on evidence.

They left a collection of medical books, called the Hippocratic Corpus, to educate physicians who came after them. Today, graduating medical students repeat modern versions of the Hippocratic Oath, a promise to treat the sick to the best of their ability, preserve patient privacy and pass on medical knowledge to the next generation.

ca 250 BCE Compass invented

A compass is a device that indicates magnetic north. So it must have been invented to help travelers, right?

Actually, an early compass was invented around 250 BCE in China to help align buildings and furnishings in keeping with the forces of nature — a technique known as *feng shui*. Some people think Mexico's Olmec people may have used a compass for the same purpose as early as 1400 BCE.

But the compass really took off with travelers. Before they had compasses, people navigated by using the Sun as a guide during the day and the stars at night. In cloudy weather, it was easy to get lost. Sailors had to stay within view of shore so they could see landmarks.

RIPPLES

With a compass, sailors could travel across seas and oceans, far from land and no matter what the weather. So people began to explore the world and to trade with other countries.

Later, scientists such as Michael Faraday (page 57) and Albert Einstein (page 72) were intrigued by the compass needle's invisible guiding force — magnetism. Their investigations of magnetism led them to new scientific discoveries.

Compasses improved navigation greatly. It wasn't until the late 1900s that a new navigational aid, the Global Positioning System (GPS), took over.

ca 250 BCE Archimedes changes math and science

According to a story from ancient Greece, King Hiero II had a new crown. It was supposed to be pure gold, but the king suspected that the goldsmith had mixed the gold with a cheaper metal. The king asked Archimedes, a mathematician, to investigate.

Not long after, Archimedes stepped into a bath and noticed that the water level rose when he got in. He reasoned that an object in water moves an amount of liquid related to how dense the object is. This gave him a way to measure the amount of gold in the crown.

Archimedes ran outside, naked, yelling "Eureka," meaning "I've found it!" When the crown was tested, it turned out the goldsmith had cheated.

The naked run is probably just a story. But Archimedes did solve many mathematical problems. He also figured out how the distance across a circle (the diameter) is related to the distance around the circle (the circumference). And he calculated the volume and area of a sphere.

Archimedes figured out how a boat's weight relates to its volume, and so how much cargo it can carry. He developed the Archimedes' screw (page 13) — a water pump that is still in use — as well as levers, pulleys and weapons.

ca 221 BCE Great Wall of China built

Imagine a wall stretching 8850 km (5500 mi.). That's about how long the Great Wall of China is.

The Great Wall is the longest structure ever built. It snakes through steep mountains, flat plains, lush grasslands and windy deserts. The Great Wall today is impressive and massive, but it started out not as one wall but as a series of walls.

About 2500 years ago, rulers in China's northern states began building walls to mark the boundaries of their territories. Messengers ran along the walls, taking notes from one ruler to another, making communication easier. But the main reason the walls were constructed was to keep out invaders from Mongolia. However, the walls were not very effective because they weren't connected. Invaders just snuck around them and carried out their raids.

Around 221 BCE, Qin Shi Huang became China's first emperor and unified all its states. The country's name comes from "Qin" (pronounced "chin"). Emperor Qin ordered that all the sections of wall be connected, and so work began on the Great Wall of China.

Building the Great Wall was grueling and dangerous. Some experts estimate that two to three million workers

died during its construction. The emperor was a cruel, tyrannical ruler, and rumors flew that the dead workers were tossed into the foundations of the wall. However, this would have made for a very unstable structure, so it's quite unlikely.

About 500 to 600 years ago, the wall underwent a major renovation. What tourists see today was built during this time. In places it's three stories tall and wide enough for 10 people to walk along side by side. But now nature threatens the wall — winds have eroded some portions, and sandstorms have buried others.

The Great Wall shows how important beauty is in Chinese culture. Graceful arches frame doorways and windows. Even the twists and curves of the wall flow elegantly.

RIPPLES

When the Great Wall was built, the Chinese believed their culture was the most important one in the world. They considered other people to be inferior. The wall kept outsiders away. It also kept Chinese people apart from the world. Behind the Great Wall, their culture developed in its own way, without influence from other countries.

To much of the world, China was a land of mystery. Inventions and discoveries made there were unknown. Over time that changed. Today, the Great Wall is China's top tourist attraction, and outsiders are welcomed warmly.

ca 100 BCE Silk Road flourishes

The Silk Road wasn't just one road, and it wasn't just about silk. It was an important network of sea and land trade routes between the East and West. Merchants first used these routes around 100 BCE to trade between places such as China and India in the East and Greece and Rome in the West. They brought goods that people in the West craved — spices, gold, ivory, exotic animals, plants and, of course, silk. And they introduced Chinese inventions to the West, including gunpowder and paper. In return, they provided people in the East with goods such as cosmetics, silver, amber, carpets, perfume and glass. The Silk Road also helped spread ideas and religious beliefs, such as Buddhism, Christianity and Islam.

But traveling the Silk Road was not easy or quick. Journeys took months or sometimes years. The road was often tough and treacherous. Bandits attacked traders' caravans. Merchants lost their way or died of starvation or dehydration in the desert. They stumbled into wars and sometimes were caught up in the fight. Marco Polo's famous account of his four-year trip to China in the 13th century CE describes the long, dangerous, ever-changing journey he made with his father and uncle from Venice to China (page 35).

Despite all these difficulties, travel and trade along the Silk Road continued for almost 2000 years. It wasn't till the Mongols lost power in China and the Ming Dynasty rose in the mid-14th century that trade along the Silk Road severely declined. The Ming emperors cut off contact between East and West. To make matters worse, the Black Death, a plague spread by merchant ships, killed millions and curtailed trade along the Silk Road.

RIPPLES

Although the Silk Road was no longer used after the 14th century, the desire for goods from the East continued. By the 15th century, the plague had died down, and European kings and queens began to send explorers out by sea to find a safer, swifter route to the East. One of these searchers, Christopher Columbus (page 40), accidentally landed in the Americas, and that opened a whole new part of the world to exploration and settlement.

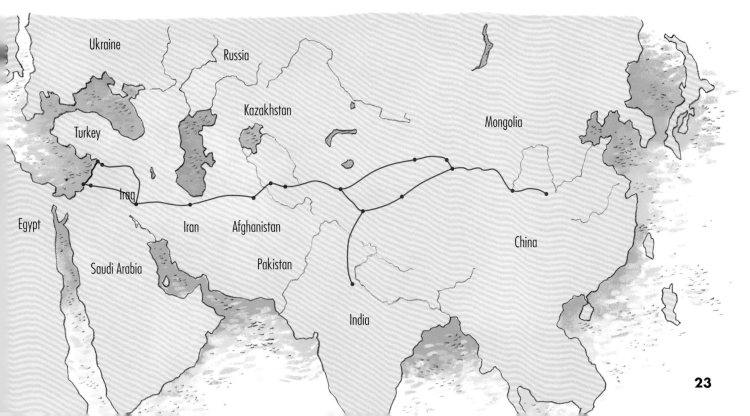

ca 100 BCE Rise of the Roman Empire

Empires don't rise (or fall) overnight — they do so gradually. That was true of the Roman Empire, which started out as a single city — Rome, founded around 753 BCE (page 18).

After Rome ousted its last king in 509 BCE, it established a republic, so that all citizens (except women and slaves) would have a say in how it was ruled. Its famous motto *Senatus Populusque Romanus* (Latin for "the Senate and the people of Rome") expressed this intention. But things didn't work out exactly that way. War and power struggles within Rome changed the republic.

Wars took a huge toll on men, resources and money. The Carthaginians of North Africa were a particular thorn in Rome's side. In 218 BCE, Carthage's general Hannibal mounted a daring attack on Rome. He crossed the Italian Alps with a large force of soldiers and elephants, surprising the Romans in their home territory. The Romans lost that battle, but the tenacious warriors hung on. The battles between the two armies continued for years, causing great bloodshed on both sides, until the Romans finally defeated the Carthaginians in 146 BCE.

Political intrigues also played a part. By 45 BCE, the Roman general Julius Caesar had conquered the neighboring Gauls, accumulated wealth and gained total control of Rome. Caesar was a dictator but also forgave his enemies, gave them good positions and expanded the Roman Empire. Despite this, many Roman senators resented his power. They thought he was destroying the Roman Republic.

The senators plotted against Caesar. On March 15, 44 BCE, Caesar was stabbed to death in the Senate of Rome. Some of the men involved in his murder had been his closest allies.

Caesar's murder intensified rivalries between the Roman generals and senators, many of whom craved power. This infighting led to the end of the Roman Republic.

Caesar's adopted son, Octavian, finally restored order in 30 BCE. He eventually declared himself Augustus Caesar, head of the empire. Rome was subsequently ruled by a series of emperors, until its power weakened when people from eastern and western Europe, called "barbarians" by the Romans, overran it. The western part of the Roman Empire fell by 476 CE. The eastern part, with its capital in Constantinople (now Istanbul), survived for another thousand years until the Turks conquered it in 1453.

RIPPLES

For about five centuries, the Romans ruled a vast empire that covered much of what is now western Europe, North Africa and the Middle East. They were great builders, especially of towns, fortifications, bridges and roads. Wherever they ruled, they created an organized system of law and government. Their achievements were an important contribution to Western civilization.

ca 5 BCE Jesus Christ is born

A new religion started with the birth of Jesus Christ. His followers believe he is the son of God, born to lowly parents in a stable in Bethlehem, in the Middle East.

The story of Jesus's life is recorded in the Bible. His followers, who became known as Christians, believe that he performed many miracles, including bringing a dead man back to life. But Jesus's main message was one of peace, forgiveness and love for others.

The political and religious leaders of the time didn't understand or trust Jesus and feared he was gaining too much power. So when Jesus was about 30, he was arrested and nailed to a cross until he died. That's why the symbol of Christianity is the cross. Jesus said he would reappear after his death, and a number of followers recorded that they saw him. Then, they reported he rose into heaven.

Christianity motivated explorers to travel and spread Jesus's story. It produced the Crusades (page 32), influenced people to start organizations such as the International Red Cross and inspired great leaders including Martin Luther King Jr. (page 97).

Today, Christianity has about 2.2 billion followers, making it the world's largest religion.

79 Mount Vesuvius erupts

They heard it first. Then the air suddenly filled with ash and dust. They couldn't breathe or see. Many could do nothing to escape. On August 24, 79, two cities of beauty and wealth, Pompeii and Herculaneum, were erased by the volcanic explosion of Mount Vesuvius.

On that day, thousands of people died in Pompeii and Herculaneum. The two cities were buried under ash, stone and lava from the volcano.

Pliny the Younger felt the accompanying earthquake and saw the volcanic eruption from 29 km (18 mi.) away. He was the first person to describe a volcanic eruption in writing. He wrote that a huge cloud towered above the area like a giant pine tree. The sea was sucked back and then forced forward in what we now call a tsunami. He described how survivors fled and searched desperately for their families.

RIPPLES

In 1748, the remains of Pompeii began to be uncovered. Since then archaeologists have found furniture, art, mosaics and even loaves of bread. The ash preserved it all. We've learned much about life in the past from these preserved remains.

105 Cai Lun invents paper

Clay, wood, leaves, silk, papyrus, parchment — people had written on these materials for thousands of years. But they all had drawbacks — they were too heavy, expensive or fragile. There had to be a better way to send messages, record ideas and share information.

In 105, Cai Lun of China tried something new. He mashed up rags, bits of wood and grasses, pressed them together, then dried them in flexible sheets. The result is what we call paper.

People in China began to write down the trades they made with each other. They traded the paper for objects, which made business more efficient. And paper allowed people to record their ideas and share them. Paper changed how people communicated and stored information.

Cai Lun's papermaking technique stayed in Asia for hundreds of years. Then, so the story goes, in 751, some Chinese papermakers were captured in a battle against Arab forces. They gave away the secret of making paper, and the technique began to spread, reaching Europe in the 1100s.

Before paper, books in Europe were painstakingly written out on parchment. This material was made from the skin of lambs, which was soaked, stretched, dried and smoothed. Preparing one book could take hundreds of lambskins. Paper was much cheaper.

Paper changed again when the spinning wheel (page 28) was invented. How? Before this invention, cloth was expensive, so clothes were worn and patched until there was almost nothing left of them. That meant there weren't a lot of rags around. But the spinning wheel made cloth cheap and plentiful, so more clothes ended up as rags. These could be turned into pulp and inexpensively made into paper.

RIPPLES

Cheap paper led to the invention of the printing press (page 38) in 1440, and that resulted in lots of books being printed. Booksellers wanted to create a market for all of those books, so people were encouraged to learn to read.

Knowledge began to spread more quickly. Now farmers and other workers had access to books and the same information that lords and scholars had. That made them feel more equal and want a say in government and issues that affected them. The idea of democracy — of everyone having an equal vote — began to spread.

In 1844, manufacturers began making paper from wood pulp instead of rags. A new industry was created to grow and log trees for paper. Today, paper made from wood pulp is used for hundreds of things, including money, packaging, documents, newspapers and advertisements.

In 1975, people began talking about the "paperless office" — they predicted that computers would end the need to print documents. But so far, that hasn't happened. We're still using lots of good old-fashioned paper.

ca 250 Golden age of the Maya

A powerful, organized and sophisticated society grew up in Central America. It was the Maya, who began to live in the Yucatán Peninsula and Guatemala area around 1800 BCE. Agriculture was key to their existence. They cleared forests to make way for crops and stored rainwater underground for irrigation. Maize (corn) was their most important crop, but they also grew squash, beans and peppers.

The Maya were also able seamen who traded goods such as honey, salt, furs, feathers and jade. And they were great builders. They constructed elaborate plazas, temples, paved roads, aqueducts, terraced pyramids, tombs, palaces and more than 40 cities — all without metal tools.

The period 250–900 was the golden age of the Maya — a time of great growth and development.

It was probably during this time that the Maya made significant advances in mathematics. They developed a solar calendar system based on 365 days. Maya astronomers traced the path of Venus, Mars, Jupiter and other planets and predicted solar and lunar eclipses. They also filled books and tablets with their hieroglyphic writings.

Maya society was organized in city states, and there were four main classes of people: nobility, priests, common people and slaves. The ruler of each city state was considered a semi-god and lived in the capital city. Smaller cities surrounded the capital and were ruled by lesser nobility.

The priests were the religious leaders. The Maya religion had many gods linked to nature. Religion was important and sometimes involved bloodletting and human sacrifice.

Commoners were farmers, architects, stonecutters and carpenters. Slaves included prisoners of war, orphans and those caught stealing.

The Maya had an advanced civilization that survived for centuries. Around 900, scientists and archaeologists believe there was a terrible drought that caused food and water shortages. Although the Maya survived these terrible times, their civilization began to decline. When the Spaniards arrived in the mid-1500s, they brought diseases, especially smallpox. They also overpowered the Maya with guns, which the Maya lacked. That further weakened an already declining civilization.

RIPPLES

Maya art and food, such as chocolate, have continued to influence other cultures. Today, archaeologists and tourists flock to Maya sites to study and marvel at the remains of this once-great civilization.

But the Maya people never disappeared. More than two million Maya still live in Central America. They have preserved much of their language, art, food, housing styles and clothing.

ca 500 Spinning wheel invented

Until about 200 years ago, women made most of the clothes for their families. First, they had to make the thread, then weave it into cloth. To create the thread, they used animal hair or plant fibers. The women realized that if they twisted the fibers together, the thread was stronger. They made the twisted thread using a hand tool called a drop spindle.

As early as the year 500, an Indian inventor mounted a spindle on its side and added a wheel. This spinning wheel allowed women to make thread almost twice as fast, speeding up cloth production.

RIPPLES

In the 1760s, a series of spinning wheels were combined to make the spinning jenny. This device could do the work of several spinners, and making fabric became even faster and cheaper.

Spinning moved out of the home and into factories. Spinning machines and looms (machines that weave thread into cloth) helped launch the Industrial Revolution (page 53).

Textile factories opened in England in the late 1700s. One was set up in Cromford Mill because there were lots of children there, and they could be paid low wages. For many years, children as young as four worked in factories, until child labor laws prevented bosses from hiring them.

ca 570 Muhammad is born

Muhammad ibn Abdullah was a merchant in what is now Saudi Arabia. He became a prophet and the key figure in one of the world's great religions, Islam.

Muhammad was born around 570 in Mecca, a city where people worshipped many gods. At about age 40, he began to reflect on his religious beliefs, often in solitude. According to Islamic belief, while he was meditating in a mountain cave, he had a revelation from God through the angel Gabriel. The revelation was that there is only one true god, Allah. This and later revelations became the core of the holy book of Islam, the Qur'an (or Koran).

Muhammad began to tell others about his revelations. At first, the people of Mecca ignored his teachings, so in 622 he and his followers left Mecca and moved to the city of Medina. This migration is called the *Hijra* (or *Hegira*) and marks the start of the Muslim calendar and the Islamic era.

RIPPLES

Within a few years, Medina and even Mecca embraced Muhammad's new faith. By the time he died in 633, a vast area of Arabia followed Islam.

Today, more than 1.5 billion people follow the Muslim faith, and Muhammad is revered as a prophet.

ca 800 Printing invented

During the Tang Dynasty in China (618–906), someone had a bright idea. Patterns were already being printed on textiles using wooden blocks carved with designs. Why not do the same thing with writing?

The earliest-known dated, printed work was made in 868. It's a Chinese scroll about 5 m (16 ft.) long that contains the "Diamond Sutra," a sacred Buddhist text. The printing on this scroll is sophisticated, which suggests the technique had probably been used for a while.

By the end of the ninth century, this woodblock printing technique was employed all over China for dictionaries and textbooks and for teaching students.

RIPPLES

Printing changed the Chinese attitude to work and status by providing access to educational materials for more people. Job success and opportunities were no longer based solely on the rank you were born into but on how much knowledge you acquired and how well you performed on examinations. Printed works helped spread knowledge.

By 1040, Pi Sheng had invented a movable-type system of printing. By 1340, texts featuring two colors, red and black, appeared in China.

The Chinese were centuries ahead of the rest of the world. It wasn't till 1440, when Johannes Gutenberg invented the printing press (page 38), that Europe caught up.

ca 800 ibn Hayyan develops scientific method

Long ago, people thought of scientists as something like magicians. They mixed chemicals and often ended up with surprising results. Without a way of accurately repeating an experiment, it seemed as if the same procedure could result in different outcomes.

It's believed that around 800, Iranian-born chemist Jabir ibn Hayyan found a way of performing experiments to make them repeatable. His technique became known as the scientific method.

What is it? Start by asking a question, then predict what will happen. "On a hot, sunny day, will I be cooler wearing dark clothes or light ones?" Your prediction, called a hypothesis, could be, "Whew! I'm afraid I'll broil in black!"

You perform the experiment, writing down each step and your observations. That way, other scientists can repeat your experiment to see if they get the same results.

The final step of the scientific method is the conclusion. You sum up your results and explain how they prove or disprove your hypothesis.

Instead of saying what they merely believed to be true, scientists could now show proof of their ideas through experimentation. And they could share their results, making science more understandable to other scientists — and ordinary people. The scientific method can link existing theories or help form new ones.

ca 800 Age of the Vikings

In 793, the Vikings attacked a monastery on Lindisfarne, an island off the northeast coast of England. That brutal raid was followed by many others, as the Vikings pillaged and plundered communities along the Baltic and North Seas.

Soon a desperate cry echoed through England, Ireland, Scotland, France and Russia: "From the fury of the Northmen, good Lord deliver us!" People quaked at the sight of the Vikings (also called Northmen or Norsemen). People never knew when they'd show up and destroy a monastery or town. Nothing was safe from these invaders from Scandinavia. In 853, they captured Dublin; in 866, York; and by 870, advanced farther into England. For the next 300 years, they marauded, looted and terrified communities. The English were so rattled by the Viking invaders that they regularly paid them off with silver.

The Vikings thought they had good reason to invade other areas. Many were farmers, but much of their northern lands were hard to farm. They wanted better land and were prepared to grab it. As for treasure and power, why not acquire those, too?

What made the Vikings so successful in their raids? Their strength was their sea power. Their sleek, fast ships, called *knorrs* and longships, could navigate shallow waters and sneak into shore without anyone knowing. These skilled sailors didn't use the compass (page 21). By the time it was around, the Viking era was drawing to a close.

With such great navigational skills, you'd think the Vikings would have explored beyond Europe. The problem was that their ships, although well suited to shallow water, were difficult to sail in the open sea.

One Viking, Eric the Red, did make a long sea journey and settled in Greenland. He was forced into it. He'd been kicked out of his homeland, Iceland, because he had murdered too many of his fellow Vikings.

His son Leif Eriksson (dubbed "Leif the Lucky") was an explorer, too, but he was motivated by curiosity. When Leif heard that another Viking sailor had spotted new lands after drifting off course, he decided to check out the story for himself.

Around the year 1000, Leif and 35 other Vikings sailed from Greenland. He and his crew crossed the Atlantic Ocean and headed down the coast of North America. They landed in what is now Newfoundland, becoming

the first Europeans to set foot in North America — almost 500 years before Christopher Columbus (page 40)! Leif even established a colony there, but the colony didn't thrive and eventually failed.

Viking sagas (tales) described Leif's adventures and discoveries. They were passed down orally from Viking to Viking, and many people wondered if they were true. Then, in 1962, archaeologists discovered the remnants of Viking houses, tools and the odds and ends of daily life at L'Anse aux Meadows in Newfoundland. These remains proved that the Vikings had come to North America, stayed for a few years and then left.

Eventually, the Vikings settled permanently in the European countries they invaded, and became traders and farmers. The last Viking battle took place in 1066, when Harald Hardrada, the Viking king of Norway, tried to conquer England. His attempt failed, and the Viking Age came to an end.

RIPPLES

The Vikings were only in North America for a brief time and didn't leave much of a mark on that continent. However, they left a huge imprint on Europe by intermarrying with the local people and sharing their culture. Many Europeans have Viking ancestors, and English has many traces of Viking words. For example, the words "Thursday," "berserk" and "outlaw" can be traced back to their language.

The Viking language, culture and traditions have become part of the fabric of European life.

1044 Gunpowder invented

Chinese chemists may have accidentally made gunpowder in 1044 when they were trying to find a substance that would give people eternal life. They realized the powder had another (and potentially deadly) use when it flared up and burned down the house where they were working. The Chinese name for gunpowder means "flaming medicine."

Before gunpowder, the bigger and stronger fighter usually won the battle. But no longer. And guns were much more accurate than bows and arrows, so soldiers no longer had to be fairly close to the enemy.

Gunpowder led to new weapons, such as cannons. The use of cannon warfare began to spread from China to the Middle East and Europe in the 1200s, along the Silk Road (page 23). City and castle walls were no match for cannons.

Around 1290, gunpowder was first used in handguns. Knights stopped wearing armor, because it was useless against bullets. Swords became obsolete, too. With a gun, a peasant had as much power as a lord. So society gradually changed. Armies were created, with infantries (gun-carrying soldiers who fought on foot). Over time, war became a job, not a sport for nobles.

Guns sped up the settlement of new lands. Pioneers could use guns to protect themselves and shoot animals for food and fur.

1096 Crusades begin

For about 200 years they fought, Christians against Muslims, for a tiny strip of land in the Middle East around Jerusalem. This was the Holy Land, where Jesus Christ (page 25) had lived and died. The land had fallen into Muslim hands, and Pope Urban II decided that Christians in Europe had a duty to win it back.

The 200-year-long series of battles came to be called the Crusades because the Christians wore a cross, called a *crux* in Latin, sewn to their clothes. There were about 10 Crusades, starting in 1096 when soldiers from several European countries, including France, Germany, Spain and England, headed east. The crusaders of the First Crusade

managed to recapture the holy city of Jerusalem in 1099. But after almost 50 years of peace, fighting broke out again, with the Muslims the winners.

The Third Crusade made heroes out of the Muslim leader Saladin and the English king, who became known as Richard the Lionheart. In 1212, teenagers from France and Germany decided they could do better than the older crusaders. But this "Children's Crusade" never made it to Jerusalem. More peace treaties and battles followed until 1272, when the Crusades ended with the Muslims maintaining hold of the Holy Land.

The crusaders were beaten, but they did come away with new weapons, better skills in battle and more accurate maps.

RIPPLES

The Crusades changed Europe in many ways.

Before the Crusades, parts of Europe were constantly at war with one another. The Crusades united the various territories against a common enemy — Muslims.

The need to feed and transport huge armies of crusaders meant there was a lot of buying and selling going on. When the crusaders captured new areas, they took over the local trade routes, which brought in money and allowed the knights to take furs, gems, silks and spices back to Europe. Crusaders also returned home with new foods, such as apricots, lemons and rice.

Traveling by land to the Holy Land to buy these exotic goods took a long time and was expensive. So Europeans took to the sea instead, which resulted in more exploration.

Crusaders also learned about fortifications. Until then, European castles had been protected by wooden walls. But fortresses in the Arab world had thick stone walls. The crusaders applied this construction idea to their own buildings.

The knights and soldiers who fought in the Crusades were exposed to Arab civilizations and took home knowledge of the more advanced Arab way of living. They learned about such subjects as science, medicine and mathematics. Europeans back home began to see the world differently.

On the Muslim side, the Crusades united Muslim groups to fight together. It also made them wary of Christians and other foreigners.

1206 Genghis Khan rules Mongol Empire

Who would have thought that the Mongols, a nomadic people who moved constantly with their sheep, goats and cattle, could conquer vast and powerful empires? But their skill on horseback, their swift and sure use of the bow, and their daring leader, Temujin, gave them control of a vast area. Their empire eventually included parts of China, Central Asia, the Middle East and eastern Europe. It became the largest continuous land empire in the history of the world.

Temujin, the son of a murdered tribal chief, grew up amid violence and poverty. Despite his difficult early life, by 1206 he rose to power and was able to unite the often-warring Mongol tribes. For three decades Temujin, who became known as Genghis Khan (meaning "Lord of the Earth"), led a cunning, ruthless and successful campaign to expand Mongol power and territory.

RIPPLES

Genghis Khan's sons carried on his work. His grandson, Kublai Khan, completed the conquest of China. Kublai moved his capital from Mongolia to Beijing and adopted a Chinese name, Yuan, for his dynasty. He was interested in new ideas, art, food and medicines. He encouraged free commercial trade via the Silk Road (page 23) and welcomed traders such as Marco Polo (page 35). But after Kublai's death, the Mongols were expelled from China. By the close of the Yuan Dynasty in 1368, the Mongol Empire had ended.

1215 King John signs Magna Carta

In 1212, a small protest led by Lord Robert Fitzwalter against King John of England mushroomed into a rebellion that would change how rulers governed around the world.

Fitzwalter and a group of English barons were disgruntled about King John's rule and spread stories about the king's cruelty. Although some of the stories were exaggerated, King John often *was* cruel and unfair. He had complete power over his people and used it as he pleased. He imposed heavy taxes to finance his wars, which he often lost, and punished people who didn't pay. He even made an enemy of the pope by seizing papal property after a disagreement. The pope was so furious he excommunicated King John (barred him from the Catholic Church) in 1209.

By 1214, King John had lost all the French territories England had once owned and was forced to return them to France. The loss of these lands further damaged King John's power and prestige.

The rebels were now ready to strike. Led by Fitzwalter, they attacked London. King John's forces couldn't repel them. By May 17, 1215, London fell to the rebels.

The barons immediately insisted on more rights, fairer laws and fewer taxes. King John refused to listen to their

demands. But the rebels would not back down. They forced the king to flee from London. His advisors begged him to make peace and agree to the rebel demands. Otherwise, they warned, England would be plunged into civil war.

King John finally gave in. On June 15, 1215, at the meadow of Runnymede on the banks of the Thames River, he made a deal with the rebels. They wanted rights and liberties for all freemen. They wanted the king to consult them before he imposed new taxes. They wanted fairer trials. They insisted that the king follow a set of written laws, the Magna Carta (great

charter), and they wanted to elect 25 men to make sure he did.

King John had no choice but to sign the Magna Carta.

RIPPLES

Although King John had no intention of abiding by his agreement, and civil war *did* break out, the Magna Carta changed England and much of the world forever. It influenced British law and, later, governments around the world. It inspired people to fight for individual rights and limit the powers of rulers and governments. It continues to be a symbol of justice and freedom.

1271 Marco Polo treks to China

In 1271, 17-year-old Marco Polo left Venice, Italy, with his father and uncle and headed for China. For four years the three traders tramped across deserts, up mountains and through exotic cities and towns. When they reached China, Marco was astonished by its wealth and the vastness of the empire ruled by Kublai Khan. The Khan liked Marco and hired him to travel around China and report back on what he saw.

After 17 years in China, the Polos returned to Venice. No one could believe that they were still alive, and the stories they told of their travels in China were almost too fantastic to be true.

When Marco Polo landed in a Genoa jail after being captured in war, he told the tales of his China adventures to a fellow prisoner, who wrote them down. Although many still questioned the truth of what Marco described in *The Travels of Marco Polo*, his book became a bestseller. To his dying day, in 1324, Marco Polo insisted, "I have only told the half of what I saw."

RIPPLES

Marco Polo's book had an enormous influence on explorers such as Christopher Columbus (page 40). It fueled their desire to find the riches of China and the East. It also attracted European interest in the exotic lands of the Orient. And despite the skepticism of many people, archaeologists and historians have proved that much of what Marco described was true after all.

ca 1277 Huygens invents mechanical clock

Back in the days of water clocks — they dripped, dripped, dripped like sand in an hourglass — timekeeping was not very accurate. That made life hard to organize.

Around 1277, a clock powered by gears that were driven by weights was invented in Europe. It was much better at keeping time than earlier clocks. Many gear-powered clocks had no numbers or hands on their faces. Instead, bells rang out the time — the word "clock" comes from the Latin word for bell.

In 1656, a Dutch scientist named Christiaan Huygens invented a clock driven by a pendulum, like today's grandfather clocks. Because a pendulum swings back and forth at a precise speed, this clock was the most accurate yet. In fact, for almost 300 years, the pendulum clock was the world's most dependable timekeeper.

RIPPLES

Clocks made things run like, well, clockwork. But they were also a big help to ocean sailors and explorers. These mariners could use a clock to figure out their longitude (their position east or west on the Earth).

Today, computers depend on internal clocks to coordinate various processes. And scientists use clocks to locate the epicenter of earthquakes, maintain the accuracy of satellite navigation systems and more.

1286 Eyeglasses invented

For a long time, people noticed that things looked bigger when seen through a curved piece of glass. So in 1286, someone thought to put two pieces of curved glass in a frame and wear them.

With eyeglasses, scholars and scientists — even ordinary folk — could keep reading as they aged and their eyesight deteriorated. Sales of glasses soared when books began to be printed around 1440 (page 38).

1337 Hundred Years' War begins

When France and England began fighting over the French throne in 1337, no one imagined how long the war would last. The Hundred Years' War changed warfare and made the French and English see themselves as separate nations.

When the war started, the most important fighters were knights on horseback. By the end of the war, they'd been replaced by soldiers and peasants with longbows. Firearms and cannons were also introduced in the course of this long war.

The Hundred Years' War didn't end until 1453, so it actually lasted 116 years. The French forces eventually won, inspired, near the end, by the French heroine Joan of Arc.

ca 1347 Black Death breaks out

By the time the bubonic plague wound down, millions of people were dead. The plague, often called the Black Death, was a bacterial infection carried by fleas and spread by rats along trade routes. Unsanitary, overcrowded conditions in cities and towns and the lack of medical knowledge made the plague unstoppable.

As more and more people were infected, law and order collapsed and there was widespread famine. This terrible combination of disease and starvation devastated much of Asia, North Africa and Europe. The plague had finally diminished in strength by 1352. But it would take years for the population of Europe to recover.

ca 1400 Renaissance begins

The Renaissance has been called a time of rebirth for Western society. When and where did it begin, and what was reborn?

Some historians say that the Renaissance began in 1341, when Francesco Petrarch, a scholar and writer from Florence, Italy, was crowned poet laureate (official poet) of Rome.

But most feel that the Renaissance didn't begin in a single year or with a single person. It was a time when ideas and achievements by philosophers, artists, writers and scientists flowered. By the 1400s, Renaissance ideas had spread across Europe.

The Renaissance flourished after a long period in the Middle Ages when writing and art from the great classical period of Greece and Rome were ignored. In the mid-1300s, scholars such as Petrarch rediscovered Greek and Roman culture and architecture and championed self-expression. Their interest and enthusiasm spread from Italy to other countries in Europe.

Soon new ideas were showing up in all aspects of life. Paintings and sculptures began to look more natural through the use of new techniques such as perspective. Renaissance art blossomed in the work of painters such as Filippo Brunelleschi, Piero della Francesca, Sandro Botticelli, Raphael, Leonardo da Vinci (page 41) and Michelangelo Buonarroti (page 41). These artists often had patrons — rich families, rulers and popes — who hired them to paint and sculpt.

Education in the Renaissance emphasized knowledge of a wide variety of subjects.

Poetry and other writing flourished first in Latin, then in Italian and subsequently in other languages. Criticism, self-knowledge and curiosity were encouraged. The invention of the printing press by Johannes Gutenberg (page 38) greatly aided the spread of new ideas.

Scientists had a harder time. Brilliant scientists such as Nicolaus Copernicus (page 45) and Galileo Galilei (page 48) proved that the Earth and the other planets revolved around the Sun. This went against the teachings of the Catholic Church, which held that the Earth was the center of the universe. Galileo's belief was so controversial that he was sentenced to house arrest and had to remain at home for the last nine years of his life.

The Renaissance lasted till the late 1600s.

RIPPLES

The Renaissance influenced the artists, musicians, scientists and writers who followed.

Many historians believe that Renaissance ideas led to the Protestant Reformation. The Reformation was a protest against the Catholic Church. Many people broke away from that religion to form new Protestant churches.

Today, we're still shaped by Renaissance ideas. We use the term "Renaissance man" or "woman" to describe someone who has accomplishments in many areas.

ca 1440 Gutenberg invents printing press

There was a great hunger for knowledge in the Renaissance (page 37). But how could people acquire new information or share the latest ideas when books had to be laboriously copied by hand? It could take months or even years to copy a single book. That made books so costly that few people had access to them.

What the world needed was a faster and cheaper way to produce books. A German goldsmith and inventor named Johannes Gutenberg came up with an invention that would fill that need.

Gutenberg was born around 1400 in Mainz, Germany. Little is known about his youth. All we know is that around 1430 he moved to Strasbourg and taught gem polishing.

Over the following years, Gutenberg worked on creating a printing press to speed up book production. Like many inventors, Gutenberg borrowed ideas from existing inventions. For his printing press, he adapted ideas from wine and cheese presses. But *his* press would apply ink to paper.

He decided to use individual letters rather than blocks made up of whole words. That way he could move the type (the letters) around to create many different words. This system became known as "movable type." He also used metal rather than wood so the type pieces would last.

In creating his movable-type printing press, Gutenberg had to meet several other challenges. He needed to make large quantities of the letters so that he could form the many words on a page. The metal letters had to be cheap to produce and easy to move and assemble into words. Further, Gutenberg couldn't use the same water-based ink used for hand printing because it wouldn't stick to the metal. His press also had to transfer the ink from type to paper with appropriate pressure, and he had to have a sufficient supply of paper. (Luckily, there was a good supply available, made from the clothing of the victims of the Black Death — see page 36.) His printing press, completed around 1440, met all these requirements.

In 1450, Gutenberg began working on printing a Bible. By 1455, he'd made 200 copies of a beautifully printed and illustrated Bible with 40 to 42 lines of text on each page. It sold quickly across Europe.

Unfortunately, Gutenberg's life wasn't going as well as his printing business. He had entered into a partnership with Johann Fust, who loaned him money to finance the production of the Bible. Gutenberg was a poor businessman and was sued by Fust. It took him years to recover financially and to gain some recognition for his invention.

RIPPLES

Gutenberg's printing press revolutionized education and culture. It led to the first mass production of books. Works of writers and thinkers could now reach many new readers, and many new people could learn to read. In less than 50 years after Gutenberg's invention, millions of books were in print, and the numbers — and literacy — grew from there.

ca 1490 Aztec Empire at peak

By the time Spanish explorer Hernán Cortés marched into the Aztec capital of Tenochtitlán in 1519 (page 43), the Aztecs had built a powerful, well-run, sophisticated civilization. They'd created a system of writing and an accurate calendar and had constructed impressive stone buildings. Their craftsmen produced intricate jewelry made of gold, silver, turquoise and jade, all without the use of metal tools.

The Aztecs were also skilled farmers. They realized that rotating crops and providing irrigation were key to a good harvest. They grew grain, vegetables and fruits.

The Aztec domination of the area had begun around 1345, when Tenochtitlán (now Mexico City) was founded. In the 1400s, the Aztecs allied with neighboring people and conquered many local tribes. They demanded huge quantities of gold, silver, fruits and textiles from the conquered people. Their rule extended from the Pacific Ocean and the Gulf of Mexico to Guatemala, San Salvador and Honduras. They had a strong administration and used tax collectors to keep their coffers full.

Religion was an important part of the Aztec civilization. Human sacrifice played a central role in their religion, which was focused on a fear of nature and the end of the world. The Aztecs believed that human sacrifices would keep nature in balance — for example, it could keep the Sun shining. Often the people killed were enemies caught in battles, but sometimes the Aztecs sacrificed their own people. Even members of sports teams were at risk — lose a game and they might lose their lives. As time went on, the rites of sacrifice became more intense, and more people were killed.

This was the world that Cortés found when he marched on the capital. How did Cortés and about 600 armed men kill more than 200 000 Aztecs and conquer this great civilization in only two years?

The Aztecs' bows and arrows were no match for the Spaniards' guns and horses. (The Aztecs had never seen horses and found them terrifying.) The heavily taxed neighboring tribes despised the Aztecs and were happy to help the Spaniards. The Aztecs also played a role in their own defeat — their practice of human sacrifice had killed off many of their own able-bodied people. And many Aztecs died from smallpox, a disease they caught from the Spaniards. Weakened and lacking weapons, the Aztecs fell prey to the Spaniards' power.

RIPPLES

Although Cortés destroyed the Aztec civilization, many aspects of Aztec culture remain in Mexico. Aztec art, music and foods, such as beans, squash, corn and chocolate, have been woven into Mexican life — and into other cultures.

1492 **Columbus reaches the Americas**

Christopher Columbus was excited and relieved. After nearly a month at sea, he and his crew had finally sighted land. And none too soon — his sailors were on the verge of mutiny.

Columbus was sure they had reached the place they'd been searching for — the fabulous East Indies. Soon he hoped to load his three ships, the *Niña*, the *Pinta* and the *Santa María*, with gold, jewels and spices. He knew that King Ferdinand and Queen Isabella of Spain, who had financed his trip, would be overjoyed. And soon he, Christopher Columbus, would be famous and rich!

But Columbus hadn't sailed to the East Indies. He had landed in the Americas, on an island in the Bahamas where there was little gold, few spices and lots of strangely (or barely) dressed people.

Despite all this evidence, Columbus would not be dissuaded. He was certain he'd landed in China or Japan.

RIPPLES

Columbus never realized that he had not found China or Japan but rather a whole new continent that would eventually yield riches even greater than those of the East. Many European explorers soon followed him and brought their religion, their ideas — and their diseases — to the peoples of this New World.

1497 **Cabot reaches the "New World"**

John Cabot was an Italian explorer who sailed on behalf of England. That wasn't unusual in those days. Many explorers, including Christopher Columbus, embarked on explorations for any country that put up money for their voyages. Like Columbus, too, Cabot was born in Italy, around 1450. He moved to England about 1495 and secured the sponsorship of King Henry VII. His mission, like that of Columbus, was to discover a route to the riches and spices of the East.

On his first journey, in 1497, his ship, the *Matthew*, left Bristol, with about 20 people (possibly including his sons) aboard. It landed at either Newfoundland, Labrador or Cape Breton — no one is sure of the exact location.

Cabot noted the abundance of fish in the area and thought he'd reached the East. When he returned to England, he was hailed a hero. In 1498, he sailed again, this time with five vessels. It's believed that he never returned.

RIPPLES

Cabot's landing place is a mystery, but he *did* make it to North America, the first European after the Vikings (page 30) to do so. His journey gave England a claim to what later became Canada. His report that the North Atlantic was teeming with fish, especially cod, led to the creation of a huge fishing industry.

1503 Da Vinci paints *Mona Lisa*

He painted the *Mona Lisa*, the world's most famous and most valuable painting, but he was also a scientist, mathematician, engineer and inventor. In all these areas, Leonardo da Vinci was far ahead of his time.

Take the *Mona Lisa*, for example. It's a portrait of a woman, hands folded in her lap, with a faint, mysterious smile. Her identity was unknown for 500 years, and even now experts are still not sure who she was. Art critics continue to examine her smile to figure out how da Vinci made it so puzzling.

The *Mona Lisa* was one of the first portraits to show a person against an imaginary background. And da Vinci was one of the first painters to use atmospheric perspective. That's the effect the atmosphere has on the appearance of a distant object — you can see his use of it in the *Mona Lisa*, too.

One reason da Vinci was such an amazing artist was that he spent a lot of time observing things. This also made him a good inventor. He watched birds and designed an early flying machine based on their flight. He also invented a parachute — just in case.

Although da Vinci hated war, he needed money, and people paid him for ideas to help them fight their enemies. He invented a diving suit (to wear when cutting holes in an enemy's boat), a tank, a machine-gun-like weapon and a fighting robot. Da Vinci's other inventions included ball bearings, which today are an essential part of many modern machines.

Da Vinci left 13 000 pages of notes (written from right to left, probably because it was easier for this left-handed inventor) and drawings when he died. Not all of the inventions he dreamed up were practical or buildable during his lifetime. But when modern scientists have studied them, they've realized that many would actually work!

1508 Michelangelo paints Sistine Chapel ceiling

Artist Michelangelo Buonarroti was *not* happy. He'd been asked to paint the ceiling of the Sistine Chapel in Vatican City, Italy. Michelangelo wanted to be known as a sculptor, not a painter. But the pope asked him, so Michelangelo agreed.

He began painting in 1508. For four years he stood on scaffolds, holding his paintbrush over his head, painting scenes from the Bible. He created more than 300 people, angels and other figures — his use of design, color and light was incredible.

Many consider Michelangelo's Sistine Chapel ceiling the world's greatest painting. Every day, thousands of tourists crane their necks to view it. And Michelangelo became famous as a sculptor, too.

1510 African slaves first shipped to the Americas

Many cultures have enslaved people whom they've beaten in war. But the slave trade that sent millions of Africans to the Americas was different. It involved kidnapping and selling people to make money for American and European businessmen.

Starting in 1510, European sailing ships arrived on the west coast of Africa from Europe full of money, guns, alcohol and other goods to trade for slaves. Africans were crammed onto the ships for a miserable voyage across the Atlantic Ocean to the Americas. It was so bad that some jumped overboard knowing they would drown.

The Africans who survived the journey arrived in Brazil, the Caribbean or the United States. There, they were put on display like animals for plantation owners to bid on them. Parents and children were separated. Most slaves worked long hours in the cotton and tobacco fields, while others cooked and cleaned in their owners' homes.

As many as 12 million Africans were enslaved. Slave traders preferred male slaves since they were often stronger and could work harder than most women. That meant that back in Africa, there were many fewer men for the women to marry and have families with. Experts estimate that the population in Africa in 1850 was only half of what it would have been without the slave trade.

In the late 1700s, people in the United States and Europe began to realize slavery was wrong. In the northern United States, people tended to be against the slave trade. However, in the south, with its large plantations, people argued that they needed the cheap labor.

Slavery was one of the major causes of the American Civil War, which began in 1861. It was finally outlawed in the United States in 1865 when the war ended.

RIPPLES

The unpaid labor of the slaves fueled European industry, especially in England. That meant there was money to explore the world and establish colonies, which is why England still has a large commonwealth.

When the slaves were freed after the Civil War, many Americans looked down on them because of their color and background. These attitudes led to decades of discrimination and erupted in racial conflicts, especially in the 1960s. Activists such as Martin Luther King Jr. (page 97) and organizations such as the National Association for the Advancement of Colored People pushed for Black rights.

Religion, language and especially music were all changed by African traditions the slaves had brought with them. Jazz, gospel and other music styles can all be traced back to African influences.

Although African-American Barack Obama is not the descendent of a slave (his wife, Michelle, is), his election as president of the United States in 2008 (page 113) signaled a new era in relations between Blacks and Whites in America.

1519 Magellan sets out to sail around the world

Explorer Ferdinand Magellan was determined to find a sea route to Asia from Spain by sailing westward. It was Spain's only choice — Portugal controlled the eastern route to the rich spice islands of Asia.

At first, all went smoothly. Magellan set out in 1519 with five ships. They crossed the Atlantic Ocean and hugged the coast of South America, trying to find a passage through the continent. The ships traveled farther and farther south, until finally …

success! In November 1520, they sailed through a narrow channel and into the Pacific Ocean. They were one step closer to Asia.

Although low on food and water and suffering from scurvy, they pushed on. On March 16, 1521, they landed in the Philippines. They were the first voyagers to reach Asia by sailing westward!

Only one of Magellan's ships made it back to Spain, and Magellan wasn't on it. He had been killed in a skirmish in the Philippines. Still, his

expedition was first to send a ship around the world and establish a westerly sea route from Europe to Asia.

RIPPLES

Magellan's voyage proved that Earth's oceans are connected, and that it is possible to sail right around the world. In his honor, the channel he discovered through South America was named the Strait of Magellan.

1519 Cortés meets the Aztecs

Hernán Cortés was brash, brave and ambitious. He'd heard about Christopher Columbus's exploits (page 40) and knew that glory and riches might be found in the New World.

At the age of 20, he sailed to the New World and worked in Santo Domingo and Cuba for 14 years. In 1519, he convinced the local Spanish commander to send him to Mexico on an expedition to claim the Aztecs' land for Spain.

Cortés assembled his ships, cannons, horses and men and allied with local tribes who despised the Aztecs and their heavy taxation.

When the Aztecs saw Cortés's fearsome arms and horses, they decided there was only one thing to do — bribe him with gold and riches! But bribes didn't stop Cortés. By August 13, 1521, after many intense battles, Cortés finally conquered the proud, wealthy and powerful Aztec Empire (page 39).

RIPPLES

More Spaniards arrived in Cortés's footsteps. Some came to conquer the tribes of the Americas, while others came to settle. They built estates and replaced Aztec religious sites with Christian churches. The Spanish left a strong mark on the language and culture of Mexico and other parts of South America.

1520 Suleiman rules the Ottoman Empire

Suleiman the Magnificent ruled the Ottoman Empire from 1520 till his death in 1566. His rule became known as the Golden Age of the Ottoman Empire.

By the mid-1400s, the Ottomans had become the major power in the eastern Mediterranean area. They had conquered the Byzantine capitol of Constantinople (now Istanbul). With their strong military and centralized rule, the Ottoman Empire expanded quickly.

Suleiman rose to power after the death of his father, Selim, in 1520. One year later, he invaded and captured the Serbian city of Belgrade. That success opened the doors to the Ottoman invasion of other central European countries, such as Hungary. The Ottomans then spread into the Middle East and even into North Africa. Soon they controlled all trade routes by land and sea from western Asia to India.

Suleiman, also dubbed "the Lawmaker" by his people, strengthened government and laws. He promoted literature, encouraged the arts and funded new architecture and the repair of historic buildings.

After Suleiman's death in 1566, the Ottoman Empire fell into a gradual decline, mostly due to incompetent rulers and changing political and economic conditions. The Ottoman Empire survived in some form until it collapsed at the end of World War I (page 76).

1526 Mughal Empire begins

On April 21, 1526, Babur, a Mughal warrior from Asia, fought the Indian sultan of Delhi. The sultan had four times the men, plus warrior elephants. But Babur had cunning and guns. He was descended from the Mongols and had inherited the fierce determination of his Persian ancestors. Although outnumbered, Babur won the battle. He soon conquered much of northern India. It was the first step in what became a great Islamic empire, covering a large part of India.

Unfortunately, Babur didn't have long to enjoy his successes. He died just four years later. His son, Humayun, took over. A likable fellow, he was also an opium addict. Within a decade, he had lost almost all the territory his father had won.

Luckily, his clever and fearless 13-year-old son, Akbar, inherited the throne. Akbar eventually extended the Mughal Empire across all of northern India. Akbar was tolerant of other religions and created a stable, unified system of government. Many consider Akbar the greatest of all Mughals.

After Akbar's death, the Mughal Empire continued to grow, but it increasingly revolved around its rulers' interests. These rulers built elaborate palaces and monuments, such as the Taj Mahal (built in the mid-1600s by Shah Jahan in memory of his wife), and taxed their people to pay for it. Power also became concentrated in the hands of local, less tolerant leaders. All this contributed to the decline of the Mughal Empire, which ended by the mid-1800s.

1543 Copernicus shows Earth orbits the Sun

Since around the year 150, people believed Earth was the center of the universe. Everything, including the Sun, revolved around the Earth, they thought.

Then in 1543, Polish astronomer Nicolaus Copernicus published a book claiming that not only the Earth but all the other planets revolved around the Sun. He based his book on years of observing the night sky and felt his ideas explained the orbits better than any other theory. Copernicus's book also stated another new theory — that the Earth spins like a top. Since people couldn't observe this rotation, they found it hard to believe.

Eventually people became upset with Copernicus's theories. In 1616, leaders in

the Catholic Church banned his book for more than 200 years because they felt it didn't follow the Bible's teachings.

But Copernicus's ideas made people realize they were part of something much bigger than just the planet Earth. His book was the beginning of modern astronomy. Today, we not only believe Copernicus's

theories but have the technology to prove them!

Copernicus began a scientific revolution, because his work inspired further scientific exploration, rather than a continuation of long-held beliefs. He gave scientists and others the courage to state their findings, even if they were different from what was accepted.

ca 1595 Shakespeare writes *Romeo and Juliet*

No one is sure who William Shakespeare really was. Many believe that he was born in Stratford-upon-Avon, England, in 1564. Others think that William Shakespeare was just the pen name used by a famous person who wanted to remain anonymous.

What is clear is that this brilliant author wrote more than 35 plays and many poems that explored universal subjects such as love, families and loyalty. Some of his plays were comedies. Others, such as *Romeo and Juliet*, were tragedies. In *Romeo and Juliet*, two teenagers from warring families meet and fall in love. Like many other plays by Shakespeare, this story of family feuds and lovers trying to

stay together despite strong disapproval struck a chord with audiences then and continues to do so today.

RIPPLES

Although the debate continues about the identity of Shakespeare, no one disputes his lasting influence on theater and the English language. His plays are still produced around the world and translated into many languages. Even though Shakespeare lived almost 500 years ago, his work continues to influence our literature and culture. He is considered one of the greatest writers of all time.

1600 Gilbert explains electricity and magnetism

The first scientist to really investigate both magnets and electricity was William Gilbert. He was an English physicist — and doctor to England's Queen Elizabeth I and, for a time, to King James I. Scientists had a lot of jobs back then.

Gilbert's interest in magnetism started when he became fascinated with the compass (page 21). At the time, England was known for its ships and explorers. Sailors depended on the compass to help them navigate. The magnet in a compass interacts with the Earth's magnetic field and shows which way is north.

But nobody really knew how magnetism worked. Christopher Columbus (page 40) thought the North Star attracted the compass needle. Others believed that mountains in the Arctic caused magnetism. Many were certain that garlic had a bad effect on compasses!

The mystery intrigued Gilbert. So he worked with ships' captains, navigators and compass makers to perform experiments on compasses. Over 17 years of experimentation, he discovered many of the things that now form the basis of our knowledge about magnets — such as how to make magnets out of ordinary metals by rubbing them with a magnet.

Most importantly, Gilbert noticed that magnetic forces often produce circular motions. That made him connect magnetism with the Earth's rotation, which led to his greatest discovery — that the Earth is a giant magnet. Gilbert realized that's why compasses work the way that they do.

Gilbert also studied electricity. Not much was known about it back then — in fact, Gilbert gave the word "electricity" the meaning it has today. It comes from *elektron*, the Greek word for amber. You may know amber as a yellowish-brown fossil or stone that's sometimes used in jewelry. More important for Gilbert, amber can be given an electric charge.

Gilbert was a true scientist. He rejected magical and superstitious explanations of results, and he didn't accept other scientists' claims without first testing them for himself. In 1600, he published his book *On the Magnet*, which showed the importance of using observations and experiments. It marked a shift in science from being a practice based on beliefs and opinions to one formed of observations and experiments.

RIPPLES

Gilbert is often called the father of electricity and magnetism. His work gave us a basic understanding of electricity and magnetism that other scientists have built on, finding new ways to harness these forces. Today, we depend on electricity and magnets in many areas of our lives.

Almost all modern appliances run on electricity, and new uses for electricity are continually being found. For example, electric cars promise a pollution-free way to get around.

Transportation, communication, medicine and technology all depend on magnets, which are found in electric motors, TVs, computer monitors, microphones and many other devices.

1607 Jamestown becomes first colony in America

Many people think that Plymouth, Massachusetts, was the first English settlement in America. It wasn't. In 1607, English settlers led by Captain Christopher Newport established a small colony in Virginia they called Jamestown. It was the first permanent English settlement in America.

An island in the James River was chosen as the site. It looked like a good, sheltered spot, but it turned out to be far from ideal. The local Powhatan Indians weren't pleased with the newcomers, and conflicts erupted. The climate was unfamiliar and uncomfortable. The water supply was poor. Some of the colonists were upper-class Englishmen who couldn't adjust to the tough conditions. Many died.

In 1608, Captain John Smith became the colony's leader. His policy of "no work, no food" helped turn the colony around. Smith was injured in 1609 and returned to England. In the following years, the colonists experienced starvation, fights with the local tribes and disease, but the colony survived.

In 1619, Jamestown became the first North American settlement to have representative government and to set its own laws. That same year, African slaves (page 42) arrived. At first they were treated as indentured servants, who could become free after a period of time. But by the 1680s, they were considered slaves with no chance of freedom.

1608 Champlain establishes permanent settlement in Canada

French explorer and mapmaker Samuel de Champlain was determined to establish a French foothold in North America. In 1604, he sailed to North America and set up a colony in Acadia on St. Croix Island (between what is now New Brunswick and Maine). When that colony failed, he established another at Port Royal in Nova Scotia. It also failed, and finally, in 1608, Champlain founded the first *permanent* colony. It was on the St. Lawrence River in a place Native people called Quebec.

In Quebec, Champlain allied with the local Huron people. He was sure they would help the French build up a successful fur trading post. Champlain even fought with the Hurons against their enemies, the Iroquois.

Champlain constantly pushed France to support the colony. Even though food was scarce, winters seemed endless, and scurvy — a terrible disease — plagued the settlers, Quebec survived and grew.

The Iroquois never forgave Champlain or the French for defeating them in battle. As a result, they sided against the French in the French and Indian Wars. By the mid-1700s France had lost its Canadian colonies to the English. Nevertheless, Quebec has retained its French culture and language to this day.

1609 Kepler publishes his laws of planetary motion

He was almost always ill and had an unhappy home life with difficult parents. Despite these difficulties, Johannes Kepler grew up to become one of the founders of modern science. His theories on how the planets moved shook the world.

For years, people had charted the paths of the planets but couldn't make sense of them. They believed the orbits were circular. Kepler ignored these ideas and came up with his own very different ideas. It takes a great scientist to do that.

In 1609, he proved that the planets' orbits around the Sun are elliptical, or egg-shaped.

That was Kepler's first law of planetary motion. His second was that planets travel faster when closer to the Sun and slower when farther away.

In 1619, he came up with his third law. It was a way to calculate both the time it takes a planet to orbit the Sun and the average distance that planet is from the Sun.

Kepler also discovered a new star, figured out that tides are controlled by the Moon and improved the telescope. What's more, this genius made his mark in the world of literature — he wrote the first work of science fiction!

1609 Galileo revolutionizes astronomy

The world's first astronomer and the father of modern physics — these are just some of the ways people describe Galileo Galilei.

Early in his career, in 1589, Galileo showed that when two objects are dropped from the same height, they'll fall at the same speed, regardless of their weight. He invented a basic thermometer in 1593 and improved many scientific instruments, including the telescope, compass and microscope.

In 1609, Galileo's observations changed how people thought of the Moon. Other people had seen shadows on the Moon, but Galileo realized these were actually mountains and craters. That meant the Moon wasn't a perfect sphere, as people thought, but rough and cratered, like the Earth.

The next year, Galileo discovered four of Jupiter's moons and realized they orbited Jupiter. That confirmed what Nicolaus Copernicus (page 45) had said — that the planets and stars didn't revolve around the Earth. Galileo's later observations of how Venus moved were more proof.

Leaders in the Catholic Church felt Galileo's theories went against the Bible. For this "crime," Galileo spent the last nine years of his life confined to his house.

Today, most people agree with famous physicist Stephen Hawking, who said, "Galileo, perhaps more than any other single person, was responsible for the birth of modern science."

1687 Newton "invents" physics

Many people have seen an apple drop from a tree. But in 1666, when Isaac Newton saw an apple fall to the ground, he saw much more. He knew he was observing an invisible force — gravity — pulling the apple down to the Earth.

Newton wondered if gravity extended into space, and if it was the reason the planets stayed in their orbits. The answer was obvious, at least to him — the planets were held there by the Sun's gravity.

In 1687, Newton summed up the way things move in three laws. These laws took the mystery out of how the planets and objects here on Earth move — things move in predictable ways. His laws are the basis of modern physics.

If that's all Newton had done, he'd still be the world's greatest physicist. But he also passed a beam of light through a prism and showed that light was made of different colors. That changed how people thought about light. Newton also created calculus, a new field of mathematics. And he added mirrors to a telescope to make it work better. Today, telescopes such as the Hubble Space Telescope still use mirrors.

What else did Newton invent? Some people say he created the cat flap to keep his cat happy!

ca 1690 Dodo becomes extinct

When Dutch travelers arrived on the island of Mauritius in 1598, they found a large bird called the dodo. As tall as a 10-year-old, it weighed about the same as a bulldog.

The newcomers brought dogs, rats and monkeys that ate the dodos' eggs. People hunted the dodos and destroyed their habitat. Within 100 years, the bird was extinct — "as dead as a dodo." The dodo became a symbol of extinction. Its disappearance was the first time humans realized they'd killed an entire species. The dodo was gone. Forever.

1751 Discovery of the commercial potential of rubber

The Olmec people of ancient Mexico used rubber thousands of years ago. But it wasn't until the first scientific paper on rubber was written in 1751 that most people realized how incredible this tree sap is. Rubber became so useful that by 1909 people couldn't get enough of it, and scientists began making synthetic rubber.

Today, cars and trucks roll along on rubber tires. And where would sports such as hockey and soccer be without rubber pucks and balls?

1759 Defeat of the French in Canada

In 1759, British soldiers won a battle against the French in what is now Canada's province of Quebec. The French left North America for good. But the win left the British with a huge debt. So Britain began heavily taxing its territories in North America.

The American colonies objected to the taxes. They had begun to see themselves as American, not British, and they rebelled (page 52). In 1776, the colonies united and became the United States of America.

In 1812, when the Americans tried to take over what is now Canada, the people fought back — they considered themselves a separate nation. That led to the formation of Canada in 1867.

1768 Cook explores the Pacific Ocean

How could a young man from a poor English family succeed in the late 1700s? By going to sea. If you were lucky, daring and smart, you might rise in the ranks. That's what James Cook did, and he rose to be a ship's captain and one of the most renowned explorers and navigators ever.

Even before he commanded his own ship, he had sailed to Canada, surveyed the St. Lawrence River and taken part in Britain's capture of Quebec. On his first voyage as captain, in 1768, he commanded the *Endeavour* and sailed around the Pacific Ocean. In the course of the voyage, he charted 8050 km (5000 mi.) of Australia's and New Zealand's coastlines and brought back exotic plants that wowed the English public. He encouraged his sailors to eat a diet of fruit, vegetables and even sauerkraut to prevent scurvy — a disease that could kill. Later expeditions would follow this diet, saving many sailors' lives.

On his second voyage, he sailed close to the Antarctic Circle and visited and charted more Pacific islands that were unknown to Europeans, including Easter Island. His third voyage brought him close to finding the Northwest Passage, a passage between the Atlantic and Pacific Oceans through Canada's northern waters. He continued to discover new lands, including the island we now call Hawaii. That was where he died, during a skirmish with the native Hawaiians, in 1779.

RIPPLES

Cook's maps of the St. Lawrence River were so good they were used for years.

His exploration of the Pacific Ocean and its islands opened up that region to further European contact. It also brought European diseases to a Native population that had never been exposed to them. Many Native people died as a result.

1776 Steam engine invented

It's hard to believe, but the need for the steam engine started far below the Earth's surface. In the late 1700s, England needed coal for fuel. The more coal people needed, the deeper the mines had to be dug to find enough. Water often flooded into these deep mines. Miners had to run for their lives or drown. Horses provided the power for pumping out the water, but it was a slow process.

What was needed was a better way to pump out the water. Stories about engines that used steam for power had been around for about 1700 years, but there were no practical designs. Then in 1712, Thomas Newcomen, a British blacksmith, created a pump powered by steam.

Newcomen's pump had a metal box, or boiler, where water was heated by a coal fire. When the water boiled, blasts of steam, alternating with jets of cold water that condensed the steam back into water, moved a piston up and down a cylinder. That powered an engine to pump the water. Unfortunately, the alternating heating and cooling of the cylinder used a lot of coal to generate just a little power.

Scottish engineer James Watt was repairing a Newcomen engine when he thought of a way to make it better. His big change was to create a separate compartment where

the steam condensed, instead of in the cylinder. That saved a lot of heat energy, allowing his engine to produce much more power.

Watt's first steam engine was installed in a mine in 1776. He marketed the steam engine by proclaiming how much work it could do and how many horses it could replace. Watt created the unit "horsepower," which is still used today to measure an engine's power. And the unit of power called the "watt" is named after him.

The steam engine soon moved out of the mines and into other industries. It played a central role in the incredible changes leading to the Industrial Revolution (page 53). Steam engines powered machines in factories, and steam trains (page 58) moved raw materials to the

factories and finished products to the buyers.

Steamships began sailing in 1807. They were faster than sailing ships and could cross the Atlantic Ocean in days, a journey that often took sailing ships several months. Since steamships could sail even when there was no wind, they were more reliable. They could keep to a schedule, which meant factories could count on shipments arriving. The pace of business picked up.

Why don't you see a lot of steam engines today? Steam engines were great for powering big things like trains and factories. But by 1821, scientists had invented a smaller, lighter engine, the electric motor (page 57), that could be used for many more things.

1776 American Revolution

The American colonies were ready to revolt. They were tired of British rule and being taxed by a country so far away. They felt they didn't have a say in government and were treated like second-class citizens.

The colonists' resentment of the British government came to a head in 1763 after the Seven Years' War, a war between England and France and its Native allies. It was an expensive war, and the British expected the American colonists to help pay for it. The colonists were enraged. They resented having taxes and laws forced on them. They were outraged that when they complained, they were ignored.

Each new tax infuriated them more. Finally, in 1773, outrage over tea taxes boiled over. A group of colonists, some dressed as American Indians, boarded three English ships full of tea in Boston Harbor and dumped the tea into the sea. The English retaliated with more laws, which the angry colonists dubbed "the Intolerable Acts."

In 1775, King George III of England declared that the colonists were in a state of revolt and ordered troops to put a stop to it. The colonists and the British faced off at Lexington and Concord, Massachusetts. These skirmishes, in which eight

Americans were killed, ignited the War of Independence.

On July 4, 1776, representatives of the 13 colonies met in Philadelphia to sign the *Declaration of Independence*. The document stated that the colonists wanted equality and human rights and were separating permanently from Britain. They declared themselves to be the United States of America. Now all they had to do was defeat the British in war.

At many times during the war, it looked like the new United States would lose. But the Americans fought back on land they knew better than the British soldiers did. And when the French threw their support behind the Americans in 1778, the tide began to turn.

The War of Independence ended in 1781 at Yorktown, New York, when British general Charles Cornwallis surrendered to American general George Washington. The Treaty of Paris formally ended the war in 1783.

RIPPLES

The War of Independence created the United States of America out of 13 colonies. In the years that followed, more land was added to the new country, and eventually, by 1959, the 13 colonies would grow to 50 states.

The themes, ideals, principles and documents of the American Revolution inspired many other nations in their own revolts and calls for liberty, notably the French Revolution in 1789 (page 54).

1781 Industrial Revolution begins in England

Until the mid-1700s, most manufacturing took place in small workshops or in people's homes. Then the steam engine (page 51) came along and changed everything.

Steam engines were too big for homes or workshops, so factories were built. England's first steam-powered factory opened in 1781 in the northern town of Manchester. It used huge spinning wheels and looms powered by steam engines to produce cotton cloth. The steam engines were driven by coal — luckily, northern England had lots of it.

The Manchester factory was one of the first factories in what became known as the Industrial Revolution. This was a big change in society, in which machines took over much of the work once done by people working with their hands. Thanks to the steam engine, Manchester began making cotton cloth faster and cheaper than anywhere else in the world. Soon it was a town of factories.

Over time, factories spread across England. New towns sprang up around the factories. Millions of people moved from farms to the towns. They were looking for work. Machines were also doing more of the work on farms, so many farm workers were unemployed.

In the towns, workers and their families — most of the children worked, too — crowded into cramped homes. Diseases spread quickly, killing many. The air and water around the factories became polluted. New laws had to be made to cover such things as sewage disposal and housing construction.

Factories themselves were often unsafe — adults and children worked long hours, and accidents were common. Organizations called unions were created to protect the workers and help make sure they earned a decent living.

RIPPLES

Before the Industrial Revolution, most people made their living doing farm-related jobs. That quickly changed — now many people worked in manufacturing.

The Industrial Revolution churned out products that had to be transported, so new roads and waterways were built. Steam trains (page 58) began moving goods by rail between the factory town of Manchester and the shipping port of Liverpool in 1830. And people had more money to buy these products. Thanks to the Industrial Revolution, average income — and population — grew as never before. So did the number of inventors, spurred on by the rapid changes in technology. Machine tools made inventing and making machines easier — machine parts no longer had to be made by hand.

Social structures changed because of the Industrial Revolution. Manufacturers and business people in the middle class became as important as people of the upper class and nobility.

England's riches from manufacturing helped it set up colonies and trading posts around the globe. The Industrial Revolution spread to Europe, North America and the rest of the world. It ushered in the modern era and the world we live in today.

1789 French Revolution

Revolution was in the air! Influenced by the American colonies' revolt (page 52) against unfair taxation and their fight for freedom and rights, the French people were ready to take on the aristocrats in their own country. They'd had enough of the nobles and clergy paying few if any taxes while shopkeepers and peasants had to pay more than their share. They wanted equality and a say in how they were governed.

To make matters worse, the poor harvest of 1788 created hardship — and more anger. Why were the French fighting expensive wars when the poor were suffering? Why were the aristocrats living an extravagant lifestyle while children starved? If King Louis XVI wasn't going to listen to demands for change, there was only one solution — revolt!

On a hot Tuesday in July 1789, a large armed crowd gathered outside the old Paris prison, the Bastille. After a battle with the guards that left more than 80 civilians dead, the rebels stormed the Bastille. There, to their surprise, they found only seven bedraggled prisoners. Nevertheless, the revolutionaries rejoiced that this symbol of tyranny and royal power had fallen.

Just before this, a group of reformers had created a National Assembly to govern France. This put them in conflict with the nobles and the king, who clung to power. The National Assembly abolished feudalism, which had prevented many people from owning land, and issued the *Declaration of the Rights of Man*. It announced that all men had a right to "liberty, property, security and resistance to oppression." Soon all aristocratic titles were abolished — no one would be called a duke or a count anymore — and church lands were seized. A democratic constitution was enacted.

But not long after, the revolution took a more violent turn. When King Louis tried to flee Paris to get away from the rebels, he was arrested. In 1793, he was sent to the guillotine and beheaded. Nine months later, the queen, Marie Antoinette, met the same fate.

The Reign of Terror had begun. The Revolution, which had started off as revolt against the tyranny and unfairness of royal rule, became tyrannical and brutal itself. The guillotine was in constant use. By the time the Revolution ended in July 1794, more than 15 000 people had been guillotined, and not all of them were royalty.

RIPPLES

After the French Revolution, a five-man conservative "Directory" ruled the country. That soon gave way to the one-man dictatorship of Napoleon Bonaparte. He ruled as emperor from 1804 to 1815.

Despite the violent turn of the French Revolution, its ideals of liberty and equality are still embraced in France and in other parts of the world. And although the monarchy was reinstated from 1815 to 1848, it ended soon after that, and France became, and still remains, a republic.

1790 Mozart composes

From the time he was six, Wolfgang Amadeus Mozart enthralled Europe with his piano performances and musical compositions. He played for wealthy and noble patrons, for other musicians and even in taverns.

Born in Salzburg, Austria, Mozart was brought up by his musician father, who guided his career. By age 8, Mozart was composing symphonies, and by 11, an opera. By 25, he had composed hundreds of pieces of music. His musical themes ranged from serious to lighthearted, and he wrote in every musical style, from serenades to concertos and opera. Even though Mozart

RIPPLES

Mozart's greatest success occurred after his death. He left the world a wealth of music that has influenced countless composers and musicians and continues to delight people around the world.

was often ill, he still wrote music quickly and constantly.

He wrote over dinner, while gabbing with friends and even while playing pool. He spent money freely and was often in debt.

Although he was a brilliant performer and composer, Mozart had trouble finding and keeping jobs. Clients found him rude and irresponsible and sometimes fired him. When he died at 35, he was penniless.

1796 Jenner develops vaccines

In the 1700s, smallpox was often deadly. This very contagious disease was spread by a virus. It caused high fevers and a rash that left permanent scars. In some countries smallpox killed one-fifth of the population. Survivors were often left blind.

A British doctor named Edward Jenner was looking for a way to stop smallpox when he noticed something unusual. Young women who milked cows often caught a mild disease called cowpox but seldom got smallpox itself.

Cowpox seemed to give them protection, or immunity, from smallpox. To test this idea, in 1796 Jenner took some pus from a milkmaid's cowpox blisters and injected it into his gardener's young son.

The boy became sick but quickly recovered. And he seemed to be immune to smallpox. Jenner had shown that one disease (cowpox) could be used to protect against another (smallpox), and that this could be done by vaccination, or injecting vaccines.

RIPPLES

Jenner's discovery led to more vaccines being developed for other diseases. Today, there are vaccines to fight diseases such as flu, malaria and rabies. In 1979, smallpox became the first disease to be completely eradicated by a vaccine.

Experts say that vaccines save the lives of more than two million kids a year. Over time, Jenner's work on vaccination has saved the lives of millions — more than anyone before or since.

1800 Volta invents electric battery

Alessandro Volta was so fascinated by electricity that, as a student, he even wrote a poem about it. As an adult, he created an electric battery by putting moisture between zinc and copper disks.

A battery stores energy and makes it available when needed as electricity. The battery led to such inventions as the telegraph (page 60) and telephone (page 66). Today, cars, cell phones, laptops and most portable gadgets depend on batteries. And the battery has inspired people to invent other energy-storing devices, such as solar panels.

For changing the world, a unit of electricity called the "volt" was named after Volta.

1809 Appert develops first canned food

French leader Napoleon Bonaparte wanted to conquer the world. But how could he feed his soldiers as they carried out his campaigns? The food they took with them went bad before they could eat it.

Napoleon offered a prize to whoever could preserve food for his army. Nicolas Appert won the prize in 1809 with his technique of boiling food, then sealing it in airtight glass jars.

Napoleon never did conquer the world, but canned food did. For the first time, armies and explorers could carry food with them. And ordinary people could have fruit and vegetables, not just in summer but year-round.

1816 Laënnec invents stethoscope

How frustrating! To hear a patient's heartbeat, a doctor had to put his ear against the patient's chest. Even then, the sound was faint. And it was embarrassing for the patient — and the doctor.

One day in 1816, French doctor René Laënnec saw kids sending messages to each other by tapping the end of a wooden beam. The wood amplified the sound.

For his next patient, Laënnec rolled paper into a tube, the same shape as the beam, then put one end of the tube on the patient's chest and the other to his ear. Later inventors made the tube flexible and added earpieces, as in today's stethoscope.

1821 Faraday invents electric motor

Do you have photos of people you admire on your wall? Albert Einstein, the world's most famous scientist (page 72), did — and his pictures included Michael Faraday, the inventor of the electric motor.

Faraday came from a poor family and didn't get much schooling. He worked as a delivery boy for a bookstore. The owner encouraged him to read, so Faraday educated himself. He later got a job with one of England's most renowned scientists, Sir Humphry Davy, and learned even more.

Many scientists in the early 1800s were studying electromagnetism — the relationship between electric and magnetic fields. In 1821, Faraday invented the electric motor, which used electricity

and magnets to provide power.

Ten years later, in 1831, Faraday discovered that if he moved a magnet near a wire, the changing magnetic field made an electric current flow in the wire. This led Faraday to invent the electric generator, which paved the way for power plants that made electricity widely available.

Faraday became the best-known scientist of his time. His accomplishments included making important discoveries in the field of light and discovering the compound benzene (an important part of oil). Many of Faraday's experiments didn't work, but he was never discouraged. He believed failure teaches as much as success.

RIPPLES

Faraday's invention, the generator, powered appliances, factories, lights and much more. Thomas Edison (page 67) opened the first full-scale power plant in 1882 — the generator it used was a large version of Faraday's. Guglielmo Marconi used Faraday's work to send a radio message across the Atlantic Ocean in 1901 (page 70).

For almost 100 years before Faraday's experiments, scientists had worked with electricity, but no one was able to make a practical invention that used electricity. Faraday put electricity to work. No wonder scientists say he was the father of the modern age of electricity.

1822 Babbage invents a computer

In 1822, Charles Babbage noticed how many errors there were in calculations of star and planet positions. This meant trouble for sailors who navigated by the stars. Babbage got to work on a machine that would do the calculations correctly.

His 1822 invention was called the Difference Engine. Then in 1837, he invented the Analytical Engine, which could perform more mathematics tasks. Babbage made detailed plans for machines that could do tedious calculations perfectly.

The machines were never finished, but Babbage has become known as the father of computing because his plans showed how machines could be designed to do math computations.

1824 Braille invented

If you were blind in the early 1800s, you had no way to learn to read. That was the problem that confronted a young French boy named Louis Braille when he went off to a school for the blind. He wanted to solve the problem, not just for himself but for other blind people, too.

In 1824, at the age of 15, he invented a system of raised dots to help blind people read with their fingers. His classmates were enthusiastic, but his schoolmasters were not. But Louis's persistence paid off, and today people all over the world use braille.

1825 Stephenson builds first steam railway

George Stephenson grew up in a coal mining village in England. His first job was to keep cows away from the coal wagons. Then he began working in the mines in a variety of jobs.

When George had spare time, he loved to tinker with engines and mining equipment. He couldn't read or write, but he became skilled at repairing the steam engines used to pump water out of the mines.

Stephenson was aware that inventors were trying to build a steam locomotive — a train car that used a steam engine (page 51) for power. He decided to try to build one, too. Like all engine inventors at the time, Stephenson had to make every part by hand and hammer it into shape.

In 1814, Stephenson finished his locomotive. Now he needed train tracks that it could run on. That was accomplished in 1825, when he built the world's first public steam railway — 40 km (25 mi.) of tracks that ran from coal mines near Darlington to Stockton, where the coal could be loaded on boats. It was the start of cheap, fast land transport.

RIPPLES

Steam locomotives and railways created jobs — lots of them. Men were hired to build railroad cars. Others built tracks and spiked them down.

Steam locomotives ran faster than horses and could carry heavier loads. That meant cheaper costs (and bigger profits) for manufacturers. The locomotives also ran to a schedule, so factory owners knew exactly when their materials would arrive or be delivered. The railroad was safer, too — it was a lot harder for bandits to rob a train than a horse-drawn carriage.

The railway also brought different items for people to buy. The more they bought, the more manufacturers made, again resulting in new jobs.

Soon passengers wanted to get on board, too. As railroads soared in popularity with passengers and manufacturers, extra cars and tracks were needed, meaning more jobs. Railways were built where no roads had gone before, letting people settle in new areas. Railways brought prosperity and change, and it all started with George Stephenson's curiosity and tinkering.

1826 Niépce takes first photographs

In 1826, Frenchman Joseph Nicéphore Niépce took the first photograph of a scene, using a *camera obscura* (a pinhole camera). Photographed from the window of his family's country house, it took eight hours of light exposure to make the image appear. It looked like this:

Niépce worked with fellow Frenchman Louis Daguerre to develop his invention. In 1839, Daguerre went on to invent the first practical photographic process, which didn't need hours of light exposure. He called it daguerreotype.

Soon other inventors such as Henry Fox Talbot advanced new techniques, and Sir John Herschel helped popularize the term "photography" in a speech to the Royal Society in London. Photography was on its way!

1842 Synthetic fertilizer invented

Dead fish, seaweed, manure — those are just a few things farmers had been putting on their fields for thousands of years to make their crops grow better. These natural fertilizers worked, although no one knew why. In the 1600s, scientists began studying what plants need to grow. They soon discovered that nitrogen is a vital nutrient. Later, scientists found that phosphorus is also very important.

Irish inventor James Murray knew that his milk of magnesia factory produced a lot of waste phosphorus. Could there be a way to use it to feed plants? In 1842, he succeeded in turning his factory's phosphorus waste into chemical, or synthetic, fertilizer.

Agriculture took another leap ahead in 1909 when German chemist Fritz Haber figured out how to make ammonia in his lab. The ammonia could then be used to make nitrogen for fertilizer. Combined with phosphorous, synthetic nitrogen boosted plants' growth.

1844 Morse demonstrates electric telegraph

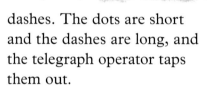

Some inventors are looking for fame and fortune. Others are motivated by a desire to improve the world. Heartbreak is what inspired Samuel Morse.

In 1825, Morse, an American painter, was working on a portrait in Washington, D.C., when he received a letter saying his wife was ill in New Haven, Connecticut. By the time Morse got there, she was dead. Morse was devastated that he had come too late. His wife's death inspired him to find a way to speed up long-distance communication.

Thousands of years ago, people communicated with others far away by using smoke signals, drumbeats or messengers. But even up to the 1800s, the fastest a message could move was the speed of the person carrying it.

In the early 1800s, experiments in electricity had shown scientists a way to transmit electrical signals through wires. But this electrical telegraph, as it was called, was inefficient and hard to use.

Morse developed his own telegraph in 1835. What was special about his system was the easy-to-use code. In Morse code, every letter or number is represented by a unique sequence of dots and dashes. The dots are short and the dashes are long, and the telegraph operator taps them out.

In 1844, Morse gave the first public demonstration of his telegraph. The invention immediately sped up communication. Messages that once would have taken days or even weeks to reach their destination now arrived in minutes.

Wires were strung up all over to carry the messages. Alexander Graham Bell used telegraph wires to carry messages when he was developing the telephone (page 66). He was actually working on a way to improve the telegraph when he invented his world-changing invention in 1876.

Morse code has saved many lives. For instance, the international distress signal is a series of three dots, followed by three dashes, then three more dots. This spells out "SOS" in Morse code. People in trouble have found clever ways to send this signal. They've flashed mirrors and turned radios on and off to summon help.

Practiced senders of Morse code each have a unique style, almost like an accent. During World War II, people receiving messages from spies could tell if the sender really was who she said she was by her style, or what Morse coders call her "fist."

Morse code allows people with severe movement disabilities to communicate. Some suck or blow on a plastic tube to spell out words in the code. Others merely blink. People who are deaf or blind can receive the code with the help of a buzzer on their skin.

1854 Nightingale revolutionizes nursing

As a young woman, Florence Nightingale decided she wanted to help people by becoming a nurse. Although she was born to a wealthy family who encouraged learning, her parents didn't approve of her nursing ambition. After all, no educated woman back then went into nursing. Nurses were poor servant girls or Catholic nuns. Hospitals were dirty and overcrowded. How could their daughter work in places like that?

But Nightingale was determined. She entered a nursing program in Germany. Then, in 1853, the Crimean War began, and Britain, France and the Ottoman Empire (page 44) declared war on Russia. The next

year, Nightingale sailed to Turkey with 38 nurses to help out. She soon realized that more soldiers were dying in hospitals than on the battlefield and pressured the military to improve the horrific conditions. She even used her own money to buy fresh food for the patients and equipment for the hospitals.

As conditions improved and lives were saved, people began to take notice. When Nightingale returned to England, she promoted her ideas in hospitals there. She began a nursing school and wrote books and articles about hospitals, sanitation and nursing.

Nightingale turned nursing into a respected profession and saved countless lives.

1856 Bessemer makes steel cheaply

Steel wasn't new — people had been making it for thousands of years. But steel was difficult and expensive to produce, until an English engineer named Henry Bessemer changed that in 1856. He created a process for the cheap mass production of steel.

Steel is made of mostly iron with some carbon. Bessemer's process involved removing impurities from the iron by blowing air through the molten metal. This and later improvements allowed large quantities of steel to be made more quickly.

RIPPLES

Steel made machinery stronger and more durable. Using steel farm equipment, farmers could produce more food. Cheap steel also made it possible to lay railway tracks across huge countries such as Canada and the United States, which helped unite the people in those countries.

Thanks to Bessemer's process, skyscrapers reach for the sky and bridges span wide rivers. Cars and major appliances are built from steel. So are bolts, nails and screws. Steel is used everywhere from offices and aerospace to ships and mines.

Today, steel is one of the most common materials in the world. More than 1.3 billion t (tons) are produced yearly.

1859 Darwin presents his theory of evolution

When Charles Darwin published *On the Origin of Species* in 1859, he changed people's ideas about nature. He said that species evolve (gradually change), creating new species, and that's why there is such a diversity of life.

Darwin began developing his theory in the early 1830s, when he visited the Galápagos Islands in South America. The finches there fascinated him.

The birds on different islands looked the same, except their beaks were different. A finch that ate grubs on one island had a long, thin beak it could poke in the ground. A seed-eating finch on another island had a short, thick beak for picking up seeds. The birds had started out the same, likely in Africa or South America, but changed over generations. This allowed them to eat the food available and so improve their ability to survive and reproduce. This process is called natural selection.

Darwin said this showed that animals adapt to their environment over time. Before Darwin, people believed species didn't change. His

RIPPLES

Darwin's theory altered how we see life on Earth. It showed that diversity in nature developed naturally and was not, as many people thought, a result of God's divine plan. This was a revolutionary idea — it changed many people's understanding not only of nature but of religion.

work made people realize that humans had also evolved and were related to apes, a shocking thought in Darwin's time.

Large ground finch

Medium ground finch

Small tree finch

Warbler-finch

1859 Lenoir invents internal combustion engine

Beginning in the early 1800s, inventors tried to create a smaller, more efficient engine than the steam engine (page 51). In 1859, Belgian engineer Étienne Lenoir built the first commercially successful internal combustion engine. Unlike the steam engine, this new engine burned its fuel inside the engine, not outside.

Here are the basics of an internal combustion engine: Fuel is forced into a small, enclosed space. The fuel is ignited, which releases an incredible amount of energy as expanding gas. That energy can make things move.

RIPPLES

Just as the steam engine propelled the Industrial Revolution (page 53), the internal combustion engine powered the 1900s. It led to such important inventions as cars (page 68), airplanes (page 71) and other engine-driven machines.

In the 1930s, engineers created the jet engine. It's an internal combustion engine powered by a turbine (a shaft with blades attached to it).

At first, internal combustion engines used coal gas, hydrogen or kerosene for fuel. In 1885, German engineers Gottlieb Daimler and Wilhelm Maybach invented an engine that ran on gasoline. The result was a much faster engine, similar to the ones most cars use today.

ca 1862 Pasteur's experiments lead to pasteurization

The next time you drink milk or nibble a slice of cheese, say thanks to Louis Pasteur. He came up with a way to make milk and cheese safe by pasteurizing them.

Louis came from humble beginnings. His father was a poor leather tanner in Dole, France. Back then, most poor children left school early, but Louis's family and the headmaster of his school encouraged him to stay in school. By the time he was 15, he was a top student with many awards. After graduation, he headed to Paris to study at a university.

The first scientific topic he tackled was how light affects crystals.

Pasteur next investigated fermentation and made a startling discovery — there are living organisms in fermented foods such as wine, beer and milk. When these foods went bad, people got sick. Pasteur discovered a process we now call pasteurization to preserve these foods and keep consumers safe.

Pasteur's interests took him in many directions. He helped stop an epidemic that was destroying silkworms and in the process became interested in infectious diseases. He explored the connection between disease, infection and microorganisms. And he began working on vaccines to prevent diseases, first for farm animals and then for humans. While Edward Jenner invented the process of vaccination (page 55), Pasteur helped develop the first vaccines.

RIPPLES

Pasteur not only helped make milk and other foods safe but also championed germ theory — the theory that microorganisms were the cause of many diseases. This discovery led to fewer infections and to vaccines that fight diseases. In Pasteur's honor, France established the Pasteur Institute, which continues to be a major force in science today.

1866 Transatlantic telegraph cable links continents

Instant communication was in the air! Since the 1840s, people had been able to send telegrams over telegraph wires. But there was no way to send telegrams across the ocean. Messages had to be sent by mail aboard ships, which often took 10 days or more. What was needed was an undersea cable to carry telegraph messages. By the late 1850s, some U.S. and British companies were ready to try just that and began making plans to lay a cable on the floor of the Atlantic Ocean.

The task turned out to be much harder than anyone had imagined. The cable snapped on the first attempt in 1857 and sank to the ocean floor. In the next year, there were more attempts and more snapped cables. Finally, in August 1858, a ship hauling cable from Ireland met up with a ship carrying cable from Newfoundland. The two cables were spliced together. Success!

1866 Mendel experiments with genes

Gregor Mendel was a monk, or holy man, with a strong interest in science and a love of nature. In the monastery where he lived in Austria, he began to grow pea plants. Mendel wanted to create new flower colors, as well as see what happened when he bred together different plants.

Since prehistoric times, people knew that plants and animals inherit characteristics from their parents. Farmers used this knowledge to improve their plants and animals by careful breeding. But no one knew how inheritance worked.

Mendel changed that. He kept track of how various characteristics, such as flower color and seed shape, were passed down through generations of pea plants. In 1866, he published his ideas:

- The inheritance of each characteristic is determined by "units" (now we call them "genes") that are passed on unchanged to the next generation.
- Each characteristic consists of two units. One unit comes from each parent.
- A characteristic might not show up in an individual, but it can still be passed along to future generations.

The importance of what Mendel discovered wasn't recognized until years after he died. Today he is known as the father of genetics.

RIPPLES

Mendel started the study of genetics — the science of heredity. For instance, scientists now know that many diseases are inherited. Thanks to Mendel's work, people can determine their probability of inheriting or passing along a hereditary disease.

His work also led to the discovery of DNA (page 92). It's the material that passes on genetic characteristics. This discovery led to cloning animals (page 109), as well as gene therapy, a process in which genes are added to human cells to cure some diseases.

Major celebrations greeted the new transatlantic cable. North America and England were now linked! Three weeks later, the cable stopped working.

By 1860, work on the transatlantic cable was suspended while the United States fought its Civil War. But by 1865, the war was coming to an end, and interest in the cable revived. After a few more failed attempts, on July 27, 1866, a cable was pulled ashore in Heart's Content, Newfoundland. The first transatlantic message was a news bulletin: "A treaty of peace has been signed between Austria and Prussia."

1869 Suez Canal completed

The world has always looked for ways to make transportation easier, safer and faster. The idea of a canal linking the Mediterranean and Red Seas was one such shortcut. It would allow ships to travel between Europe and Asia, bypassing Africa.

The canal project was organized by a French developer named Ferdinand de Lesseps. Work began in 1859 and was completed 10 years later in 1869.

At first, the Suez Canal was owned by France and Egypt. In 1875, Egypt sold its part of the canal to the English. Then, in 1956, President Gamal Nasser of Egypt nationalized the canal, making it the property of Egypt. Today, it remains under Egypt's control.

Old route —
Canal route —

1876 Refrigerator invented

In 1876, German engineer Carl von Linde discovered a process for liquefying gas to make it cold. Later, he and other inventors figured out how to use the cooled gas to keep food cold. Up until then, people had relied on ice or snow to stop food from spoiling.

At first, von Linde and others used toxic gases. But as time went on, they found safer gases, and refrigerators moved into people's homes.

Refrigeration made it possible to ship foods long distances. Now people could enjoy new foreign foods, as well as fruits and vegetables all year round.

1876 **Bell invents telephone**

Alexander Graham Bell may not have been the first person to come up with the idea of sending sound over a wire, but through persistence and ingenuity, he was the one that made it happen. And, as with many inventors, luck played a part.

Bell was a teacher of the deaf in Boston. He was also an amateur scientist who hoped to invent a "harmonic telegraph" — a device that could transmit more than one message at a time across a telegraph line. But Bell soon realized he could invent something even more useful and revolutionary — a way to send voices over a wire.

On June 2, 1875, Bell and his assistant, Thomas Watson, were working in different rooms. Watson accidentally sent a sound through a wire. Bell heard it and dashed over. A sound had been sent electrically for the first time! Bell and Watson had made a breakthrough!

An even more dramatic moment came on March 10, 1876. According to reports, Bell and Watson were working in different rooms again when Watson heard Bell's voice. Bell had transmitted his voice over a wire! Communication was about to change in a whole new way.

RIPPLES

At first, people thought the telephone was a gimmick with no practical use. But when Bell won a prize at an 1877 exhibition of new inventions, people began to appreciate his new device. By the time Bell died in 1922, the telephone was common in many households. Telephones have been primary tools of communication ever since, although the kinds of phones we use keep changing. New phone devices such as cell phones (page 100) and smartphones continue to be designed, but the phone industry started with the insight and determination of Alexander Graham Bell.

1878 Fleming establishes standard time zones

Once upon a time, every town ran on its own time. When you traveled between two places, even ones quite close together, you had to keep changing your watch to local time. For railroads, that was a big scheduling headache.

In 1878, a Canadian engineer named Sandford Fleming came up with a simple solution. He suggested dividing the world into 24 time zones, with each zone using the same time throughout and varying from neighboring zones by one hour. In 1884, a conference decided that the time in Greenwich, England, would be the basis for setting all the other time zones. We still use Fleming's system of standardized time zones today.

1880 Edison invents lightbulb

Scientists had been working for nearly 100 years to create a lightbulb. But their bulbs burned out too quickly to be of practical use. Then, in 1878, American inventor Thomas Edison took up the challenge.

Even as a young boy, Edison was curious about how things worked. He wondered if it was the worms birds ate that enabled them to fly. So Edison persuaded a friend to eat some worms. But she didn't fly — she got sick!

When he was a teenager, Edison learned how to operate a telegraph. Then he came up with an idea for making telegraph equipment work better. Soon Edison set up a workshop where he could build more inventions.

Edison knew that light bulbs glow when electricity flows through a thin wire inside called a filament. This filament resists the electricity flowing through it. The resistance makes the filament heat up and glow — it changes electrical energy into light energy.

Metals, hair, wood — Edison made filaments out of many things. His first lightbulbs lasted just 40 hours. But in 1880, he took out a patent for a lightbulb with a carbon filament that gave more than 1500 hours of light.

It had taken Edison a lot of work to make a truly useful lightbulb, but he never became discouraged. "We now know a thousand ways not to build a lightbulb," he said. But perhaps his most famous quote was, "Genius is 1 percent inspiration and 99 percent perspiration."

RIPPLES

Before the lightbulb, people lit their homes with candles, oil lamps and gas lamps. All these light sources were smoky and could start fires. Electric lights were not only safer but they let people stay up later and made streets brighter and safer at night. Factories could be open longer, which led to greater production — and longer work hours.

1885 Benz builds first car

Once the internal combustion engine (page 63) was invented, engineers began working on ways it could be used to power a carriage — a horseless carriage.

German engineer Karl Benz began building a three-wheeled vehicle with wire wheels, like a bicycle, and an engine between the rear wheels. He finished his Motorwagen (we call it a car) in 1885. The company today that bears his name, Mercedes-Benz, is the world's oldest car manufacturer.

1893 Women get the vote

It took many years and fierce determination for women to win the right to vote.

For centuries, a woman's job was to take care of her home and family. Men held political and economic power, while women were not even allowed to vote.

Some women, especially those who were wealthy, wielded power behind the scenes. And a handful of women of royal birth, such as England's Queen Elizabeth I and Queen Victoria, successfully governed their countries. But ordinary women had no real power.

That started to change in the mid-1880s as women began to attend universities, work outside the home and lead the fight against alcohol.

Despite years of struggle in many countries, such as England and the United States, it was New Zealand's women, led by Kate Sheppard, who first pushed past the strong and sometimes underhanded opposition of their male opponents in parliament. In 1893, New Zealand became the first country to grant women the right to vote.

1895 Röntgen discovers X-rays

On November 8, 1895, German scientist Wilhelm Röntgen was shooting electricity through a tube filled with gas at very low pressure. The tube produced a fluorescent glow, as he expected.

Then Röntgen wrapped heavy black paper around the tube. He was fascinated to see that rays were somehow escaping through the heavy paper. What were these rays — light? particles? Röntgen didn't know, so he called them X-rays — "X" stands for "unknown." Some people called them Röntgen rays.

Röntgen was so excited by his discovery that he ate and slept in his lab over the next few weeks as he investigated the X-rays. He realized that the rays could pass through most substances and cast shadows of solid objects on photographic film. For instance, when he held his wife's hand in the path of the rays, he created an image of the bones inside — the invisible rays had passed through her skin! The image hit the front page of newspapers around the world, shocking and amazing people.

Today, X-rays are used in medicine to examine broken bones, tumors and more. They're also involved in everything from airport security to art, where X-rays are used to scan paintings to see if they're fakes.

1898 Curie discovers two new elements

When 24-year-old Maria Sklodowska left Poland for Paris in 1891, she never dreamed she'd one day win the highest award in the scientific world, the Nobel Prize, and not once but twice.

In Paris, Maria studied physics and mathematics. She also met and married fellow scientist Pierre Curie and became Marie Curie.

The Curies worked in a dark, dingy shack, trying to find out more about materials that give out rays of energy. Wilhelm Röntgen had discovered X-rays in 1895 (above), but not much was known about these mysterious rays or the radioactive materials they came from. In 1898, Marie and Pierre isolated two new elements — polonium and radium. (Elements are the building blocks of matter.) That amazing discovery earned them a Nobel Prize for physics in 1903. Marie Curie was the first woman to achieve that honor.

After Pierre's tragic death in an accident, Marie kept working and in 1911 was awarded her second Nobel Prize, this time in chemistry.

RIPPLES

Marie Curie proved that women could succeed in science if given the opportunity. Her tenacity and passion have inspired other women to enter scientific studies.

1900 Television invented

The first time the world heard the word "television" was in 1900. Russian scientist Constantin Perskyi used it to talk about the technologies scientists were testing to try to transmit pictures.

One of those scientists was Paul Nipkow of Germany, who used a spinning disk to change an image into electrical impulses that could be transmitted. In 1926, Scottish inventor John Logie Baird gave the world the first true demonstration of television when he transmitted black-and-white images that moved.

Philo Farnsworth, an American inventor, demonstrated the world's first working television system using cathode ray tube technology in 1928. He'd had the idea back in 1921 — when he was just 15! His technology was immediately popular, and by the late 1940s, TVs were popping up in living rooms all over the world. By the late 1960s, color TVs were gaining in popularity.

RIPPLES

Television brought the world into people's homes. Today, almost every home in North America has a TV. You can choose plasma television, flat-screen, high-definition or 3-D. And you can watch television shows in cars or on computers or cell phones. Will these electronic gadgets replace the TV? Time will tell.

1901 Marconi sends radio signal across Atlantic

It was just the letter "S" in Morse code (page 60), and it was hard to hear. But on December 12, 1901, that "S" was the first radio signal sent across the Atlantic Ocean, from Poldhu, England, to St. John's, Newfoundland.

In the late 1800s, scientists had sent radio messages across short distances, but it wasn't until 1895 that Guglielmo Marconi, an Italian electrical engineer, built a system that could transmit signals over longer distances. His 1901 transmission across the Atlantic was the farthest ever.

After the transatlantic transmission, the next big step was figuring out how to make the radio waves carry more than just dots and dashes. Canadian inventor Reginald Fessenden invented a way to transmit voice and music and in December 1906 made the first radio broadcast.

RIPPLES

Before radio, people received most of their news from newspapers and magazines. Radio broadcasting sped up news delivery. People clustered around their radios to hear the latest — and to be entertained by the singers and actors of the day.

Today, radio waves are behind such conveniences as microwave ovens, garage door openers, cell phones and GPS receivers.

1903 Wright brothers fly first airplane

Bone-chilling winds blew over the dunes near Kitty Hawk, North Carolina. Nervously, American inventor Orville Wright made last-minute adjustments to the *Flyer*. Then he signaled to his brother Wilbur, standing nearby, that he was ready to take off.

The last time the *Flyer* had launched, it had smashed to the ground, and Wilbur, who'd piloted it, had barely escaped injury. They'd repaired it and were ready to try again.

What would happen this time? No wonder Orville felt jittery. After all, people had dreamed of flying for centuries. But it wasn't until the mid-1800s that inventors began building gliders. These flying machines depended on the wind to fly. What Orville and Wilbur were trying to create was a flying machine that had an engine for power and a system for pilot control.

Finally, Orville released the anchor and the airplane took off into the air. The *Flyer* was in the air for only 12 seconds, and Orville flew just 36 m (120 ft.), but it was enough to put them in the record books. On December 17, 1903, the Wright brothers had made the first-ever controlled, powered flight.

The Wrights were unlikely inventors. They had only high-school education and no other special training. But when the brothers were kids, their parents had encouraged them to investigate whatever interested them. As well, the Wright family didn't have much money, so Wilbur (the older brother) and Orville made and repaired their own toys. That gave them lots of building experience.

Like most famous inventors, both brothers were good at observing their experiments and learning from them. They kept careful records. And, unlike some brothers, these two worked well together. Wilbur had a strong drive to succeed, and Orville had a talent for inventing. They were determined, creative and imaginative — like all great inventors.

RIPPLES

Many people think the airplane is the greatest invention ever. Bill Gates, world-famous computer whiz, said, "The airplane became the first World Wide Web, bringing people, languages, ideas and values together."

Transportation sped up as airplanes were used to deliver people and goods at first short distances and then around the world. Now people cross the Atlantic Ocean in hours instead of days, and parcels move around North America overnight. Flight also changed warfare. In 1915, during World War I (page 76), the first real fighter airplane appeared.

Planes became jet propelled in 1939. Then, in 1969, a spacecraft flew to the Moon — and the astronauts carried with them fabric and wood from the Wrights' first airplane. Jets and rockets are both grandchildren of the Wrights' *Flyer*.

Today, planes fight forest fires, fly supplies into faraway areas, survey land and more. And it all started with one 12-second flight back in December 1903.

1904 Digging the Panama Canal

COSTA RICA

PANAMA

Panama Canal

Panama City

There was great excitement when French developer Ferdinand de Lesseps began coordinating the building of the Panama Canal in 1881. De Lesseps had successfully completed the Suez Canal (page 65), and he was confident he could construct this canal, too. It would save shipping time by cutting through the country of Panama and linking the Atlantic and Pacific Oceans. When it was finished, ships wouldn't have to make the long journey around the tip of South America.

But the Panama Canal was a much more complicated project than the Suez Canal.

The French faced endless engineering and machinery problems. The rocky terrain and the rivers crossing the canal site proved more challenging than the flat, sandy soil of Suez. Mudslides slowed work down. But worst of all, many workers died of malaria or yellow fever, and no one knew how to stop them from getting sick.

1905 Einstein discovers $E=mc^2$

Most people don't know what $E=mc^2$ really means, but it's still the best-known equation ever. German physicist Albert Einstein came up with it in 1905.

$E=mc^2$ says the energy (E) in an object is equal to its mass (m) multiplied by the speed of light (c), then multiplied by the speed of light again. The speed of light is 299 330 km/sec. (186 000 mi./sec.), so that's a large amount of energy.

When Einstein devised the equation, he wasn't working in a lab or at a university. Although he'd studied physics at university, Einstein had been such a difficult student that none of his professors would help him find work. Instead, he had an office job. But in his spare time, he performed what he called "thought experiments," testing theories and experiments in his mind. Other scientists had discovered that mass and energy were related, but Einstein was the first to show exactly how.

Einstein is considered the father of modern physics and the most famous scientist ever. No wonder. The same year he published a paper describing $E=mc^2$, he published three other articles that were equally

RIPPLES

The equation $E=mc^2$ led to many advances and inventions, including nuclear power, radiation therapy to treat cancer and gamma-ray scans to check out bones. The equation also calculated the amount of energy that would be released by the atomic bomb (page 89).

important to the world of physics. He was only 26 years old at the time. Einstein knew he didn't have the experience of older scientists, but he believed that "imagination is more important than knowledge."

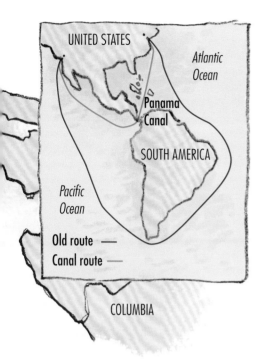

UNITED STATES

Atlantic
Ocean

Panama
Canal

SOUTH AMERICA

Pacific
Ocean

Old route —
Canal route —

COLUMBIA

the French-led venture went bankrupt.

It wasn't till 1904, after Panama declared independence from Colombia, that the United States took over the canal project. U.S. president Theodore Roosevelt was convinced that a canal was vital to American shipping and military interests.

It took another 10 years and the work of some 40 000 men for the canal to be completed. Luckily, by then scientists and doctors realized that mosquitoes spread malaria and yellow fever, and fewer workers died of disease. The United States also used better equipment and more engineers than the French had. They built houses, schools, sewers and

De Lesseps, who was not an engineer, had underestimated the difficulties surrounding the project. After spending millions of dollars and losing more than 20 000 men to disease,

hospitals near the canal site.

They decided that the canal would be built with locks — huge gates that could be opened or closed to allow ships to be raised or lowered to adjust to the canal's various water levels. The Panama Canal locks are still the largest anywhere in the world.

1907 Baekeland invents plastic

When plastic was introduced in 1907, it was the first completely synthetic material ever made. It was invented by Belgium chemist Leo Hendrik Baekeland.

Unlike natural materials such as wood or stone, this new human-made material could be dyed any color and molded into any shape. And it could withstand heat, acid and weather. Baekeland called it Bakelite and used the hard, dense material to make everything from engine parts to jewelry.

Scientists went wild experimenting with plastics. In 1908, Swiss chemist Jacques E. Brandenberger invented cellophane, a thin, transparent sheet ideal for food packaging. When plastic vinyl was invented in 1926, no one really knew what to do with it. Today, it's one of the most widely used plastics in the world. Thanks to vinyl's chemical structure, it can be turned into anything from raincoats to appliances.

Adhesive tape — another plastic spin-off — began holding things together in 1930. Nylon — yet another plastic — was created in 1938 and was first used for toothbrush bristles. Two years later it was turned into women's stockings and launched a trend that still continues. Scientists continue to create new types of plastic. For instance, the plastic Starlite can survive even a laser beam or blowtorch.

1909 Peary reaches the North Pole

Did he or didn't he? That's the question historians and scientists have asked about Robert E. Peary's claim that he was first to reach the North Pole. Even though the *New York Times* reported that he'd reached the North Pole in September 1909, it's not clear what really happened. A week earlier, the *New York Herald* had proclaimed that Frederick A. Cook had discovered the North Pole a year before Peary.

To complicate matters further, the North Pole lies on drifting ice and is constantly moving. It's tricky to know if you're actually on it. Even Cook and Peary weren't sure. Cook wrote that he and his men determined they were at a spot "as near as possible to the pole." According to Peary's companion on the expedition, Matthew Henson, Peary said, "I do not suppose that we can swear that we are exactly at the Pole."

RIPPLES

For a long time, Peary's claim won out over Cook's. (It didn't help Cook's case that he was jailed for mail fraud in 1923.) But in 1988, a *National Geographic*-sponsored review of the records cast new doubt on Peary's claim. As for Cook, the evidence isn't conclusive there, either.

The first undisputed overland journey to the North Pole was finally made in 1968 by a party on snowmobiles led by Ralph Plaisted.

1911 Art goes abstract

In 1911, Russian artist Wassily Kandinsky created the first painting that was purely abstract. Colorful swirls and lines covered the painting he called *Picture with a Circle*.

Up until then, artists created paintings that showed recognizable objects. Some paintings looked almost like photos. These are called "representational" paintings. Then artists began to create works that were less realistic. These were called "abstract," but the objects were still recognizable. Kandinsky and others took art a step further.

More and more artists of the time, including Pablo Picasso from Spain and Piet Mondrian of the Netherlands, were experimenting with abstract art. They wanted to find new ways to express their emotions and use their imaginations.

Abstract paintings changed how people look at art. When you look at a realistic painting, you can recognize the objects and figures and appreciate the story the painter is telling. But abstract paintings are sometimes just designs and colors. They're harder to understand than realistic paintings.

Art — including sculpture and music — was no longer just beautiful and decorative. Now it challenged viewers to think about art and consider what it meant to them.

1912 *Titanic* sinks

On April 14, 1912, a cool, star-studded night, the *Titanic* was on its way from Southampton, England, to New York City when it hit an iceberg in the middle of the Atlantic Ocean. The massive, elegant ship thought to be unsinkable began to sink.

It happened so quickly that there was barely time for passengers to get to the lifeboats. And there weren't enough lifeboats for all 2224 passengers and crew.

One ship at sea that night, the *Carpathia*, offered help, but it would take three hours to reach the stricken ship. In the meantime, the *Titanic* passengers who made it into lifeboats watched in horror as the ship split in two and sank.

The *Carpathia* reached New York on April 18 with the *Titanic*'s survivors on board. Many famous and wealthy people had died on the ship. Many poor immigrants who were sailing to America for new opportunities perished, too. In all, more than 1500 passengers and crew died.

1913 Bohr explains the atom

For a long time, scientists had been trying to understand the atom, the basic unit of all matter. When Niels Bohr, a Danish physicist, announced in 1913 that the atom had a nucleus (center) around which tiny particles called electrons orbited, he answered many questions that had puzzled physicists.

More than 100 years earlier, British scientist John Dalton had said that everything was composed of atoms and that there were no smaller particles. But in 1897, another English scientist, J. J. (Joseph John) Thomson, discovered even smaller particles — now called electrons. Electrons, Thomson said, had a negative charge and were scattered throughout the positively charged atom.

Then, in 1909, Ernest Rutherford (page 79) realized that Thomson's description wasn't quite right. Rutherford discovered that each atom had a center. It was positively charged and made up most of the mass of the atom.

Bohr's new idea was that the electrons orbited the atom's nucleus in precise paths, much as the planets orbit the Sun. With just a few improvements, Bohr's theory of atomic structure is still used today. That's why many people say Bohr is one of the most important scientists of the 20th century.

1914 World War I

World War I was sparked by the 1914 assassination of Archduke Franz Ferdinand of Austria-Hungary and his wife by a Serbian activist. But the seeds of the horrific four-year conflict that engulfed and devastated much of the world were sown years earlier.

The countries of Europe had made a tangled web of alliances, but there were ongoing territorial disputes. France wanted the coal-rich Alsace-Lorraine area back from the Germans — they had lost it in the Franco-Prussian War of 1870–1871. Germany wanted greater power and influence. Russia worried that Austria wanted to annex (take over) Serbia. The tsar (ruler) of Russia hoped that war would unify his country and stop talk of political change.

By the time Archduke Ferdinand was killed, many European countries were preparing to go to war. The Allied Powers (mainly France, Russia, Britain and its dominions — Australia, Canada, New Zealand and South Africa) stood together against the Central Powers (Germany, Austria-Hungary and eventually the Ottoman Empire).

In a strange twist, many of the rulers of these countries were related. King George V of England was the first cousin of Kaiser Wilhelm II of Germany and Tsar Nicholas II of Russia. Because they were cousins, no one thought they would go to war. But they did.

The war started when Austria-Hungary invaded Serbia on July 28, 1914. At first, no one thought it was going to be a long war. It began with optimism, dreams of battlefield glory and national fervor. On August 1, Germany, an ally of Austria-Hungary, declared war on Russia. On August 3, Germany declared war on France and invaded Belgium. The Germans hoped that a decisive victory over France would end the war quickly. But the Germans were stopped by the Allied forces at the Battle of the Marne.

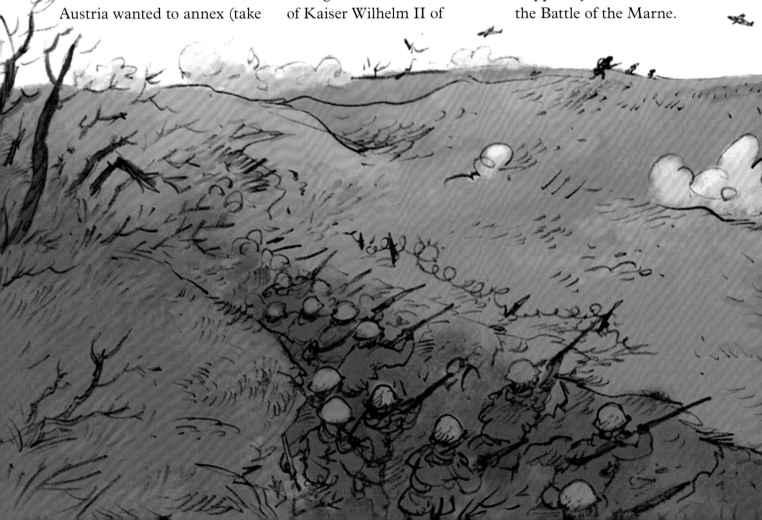

A new front opened up when the Ottoman Empire entered the fray. Russia left the war in 1918 during the Russian Revolution (page 78). The United States was neutral until 1917, but it helped supply the Allied forces with arms and materials.

The war was an ever-changing, slow-moving series of attacks and counterattacks, small battles and larger ones, with no one winning decisively. Much of the war was spent slowly picking off the enemy, a few soldiers at a time and waiting for the next skirmish. Many soldiers died of disease or sniper bullets while they were holed up in filthy, rat-infested trenches waiting for the next battle or enemy encounter.

By 1917, the Allied forces were running low on supplies and men. Many had died in the daily encounters across the "no-man's-land" that separated the opposing forces. The Allies hoped that the Americans would enter the war and assist them with soldiers and supplies. America finally joined the Allies in April, after German submarines sank U.S. merchant ships and the Zimmerman Telegram was intercepted. It revealed that Germany was trying to get Mexico to join them, which would have been a big threat to the United States.

The German army was close to defeat by August 1918 after a series of prolonged, intense battles with the Allies. The Germans agreed to an armistice (end of fighting) on November 11 and were forced to retreat within their borders.

RIPPLES

When World War I ended officially on November 11, 1918, more than 37 million soldiers were dead or wounded. It was known for its brutal trench warfare. Millions of civilians died, too, through starvation, disease or military action.

People hoped it was the "war to end all wars," but 21 years later another world war broke out (page 86). Even the League of Nations, established after World War I to settle disagreements peacefully, was unable to keep the peace.

1917 Russian Revolution and rise of communism

Russia was in revolt! Years of anger and frustration toward the tsars (rulers) of Russia triggered a series of revolutions.

The tsars had enormous wealth, while much of the Russian population lived in poverty. The desire to end this injustice increased after the disastrous Russo-Japanese war of 1905. The Russians suffered a humiliating defeat, and there were terrible food shortages. When poor Russians protested, the tsar's troops fired on them. Anger against the government was further fueled by the army's huge losses and the terrible conditions the Russian people lived through during World War I (page 76). New ideas were also filtering into Russia, including the revolutionary ideas of Karl Marx. His book

The Communist Manifesto called for the working class to rise up against the wealthy and create a society of equality between the rich and poor.

Tsar Nicholas stepped down in March 1917, and soon Vladimir Lenin and the Bolshevik party seized power. Lenin used Marx's ideas to promote his Communist vision for Russia. But the Bolsheviks controlled only a small part of the vast country, and many groups opposed them.

A civil war soon broke out between the Bolshevik "Reds" and their opposition, the "Whites." During that conflict, many Russians died of starvation, disease or execution and during pogroms (organized persecution of Jews). Many fled to safety in other countries. The Russian economy was in shambles.

In March 1918, the Bolshevik government signed a treaty with the Germans to end Russia's involvement in World War I. Although the treaty cost Russia dearly in land and population, it helped the Bolsheviks consolidate power.

The Bolsheviks controlled the two largest cities, Moscow and Petrograd (now Saint Petersburg). They were also popular with the peasants, mainly because they promised the peasants land. By 1921, Lenin and the Bolsheviks had triumphed. Russia was firmly under their control. In 1922, Russia became known as the U.S.S.R., or Soviet Union.

RIPPLES

The Bolshevik government took tight control of the country and enforced its policies harshly. It would take years for the country to recover from the Revolution, World War I and civil war. Eventually, the Soviet Union became one of the world's superpowers, second only to the United States. Communist control and a government-run economy lasted until the 1990s, when the Soviet Union broke apart into a federation of 15 republics.

1917 Rutherford splits the atom

New Zealand physicist Ernest Rutherford was already famous for his work with atoms (page 75). He knew that an atom has a nucleus (center) with a positive charge and that the nucleus is surrounded by tiny negative particles called electrons.

In 1916, Rutherford was experimenting with radioactive material. A year later he discovered he could break up the nuclei of nitrogen atoms by firing radioactive particles at them. The nuclei fragments moved incredibly fast and released a huge amount of energy. This is called a nuclear reaction.

Rutherford became the first person to split an atom — that's how most people describe his achievement, but more accurately, what he did was split the nucleus of an atom. As well, when he split the atom, he discovered and named the proton, a positively charged particle in the nucleus of the atom.

People now call Rutherford the father of nuclear physics. His work opened doors to new ideas in physics and to the development of the nuclear power industry.

What Rutherford could not have foreseen was that splitting the atom would also lead to the creation of the nuclear, or atomic, bomb (page 89), which destroyed the Japanese cities of Hiroshima and Nagasaki in 1945.

1918 Fatal flu kills millions

It was the most famous and deadliest epidemic in the world's history. Between 20 and 50 million people died from the 1918 influenza, or about 1.1 to 2.8 percent of the world's population.

Some people think the epidemic started in a military camp in the U.S., in Kansas, and troops brought it over to Europe. But it was called the Spanish flu because Spain was the first country to report serious attacks of the illness. It soon spread all over the world.

Most flus kill only about 0.1 percent of the people they infect, but this one was deadlier — it killed more than 2.5 percent of infected people. What made it so deadly? Scientists still don't know, but it was very infectious and its symptoms were incredibly severe. Unlike other flus, which tend to kill very young and very old people, the 1918 flu killed many people aged 20 to 40.

Public meetings were canceled to prevent people from gathering and spreading the flu virus. Hockey's Stanley Cup final has only ever been canceled once, and that was in 1919 when

too many of the players came down with the Spanish flu for the teams to play.

Doctors hope to learn more as they analyze samples of old, infected tissue and study its DNA (page 92). They want to prevent similar deadly outbreaks in the future.

1920 Carver revolutionizes agriculture

As a professor of agriculture in Tuskegee, Alabama, George Washington Carver saw how hard life was for Black farmers. Most grew cotton, which takes more nutrients out of the soil than other crops. Each year, the soil produced less cotton.

So Carver encouraged farmers to grow cotton one year, and then the next year plant peanuts or soybeans, which put nutrients back into the soil. This is called crop rotation, and it revolutionized farming in the southern United States by liberating famers from their dependency on cotton.

Carver also invented more than 300 products from peanuts (including pickles, shampoo and fruit punch) and 125 from sweet potatoes (such as flour, ink and glue) to ensure a need for the crops. (Most people assume Carver created peanut butter, but it was invented in 1884 by Canadian doctor Marcellus Gilmore Edson.)

In 1920, Carver was a guest speaker for the United Peanut Associations of America. To get to the meeting, he had to take the freight elevator — the regular one was for White people only. Despite this racial insult, Carver dazzled the audience. He helped southern peanut farmers again the next year when he gave an incredible presentation to a group of politicians. They were so fascinated by Carver's work that they passed a law to help the farmers.

1922 King Tut's tomb discovered

If it hadn't been for a car accident, King Tutankhamen's tomb might not have been found, and we might never have learned about a young and little-known Egyptian pharaoh who lived more than 3000 years ago.

It all started in 1901 when Lord Carnarvon of England, who loved racing around in the newly invented car, had an accident. His doctors advised him that the damp English climate wasn't good for his recovery, so Carnarvon sailed to Egypt in 1903 to recuperate in the warm desert climate.

There, he became fascinated with archaeology and ancient Egypt. But Carnarvon was no expert in the field, so he hired someone who was — Howard Carter.

Carter knew that artifacts bearing the name of Tutankhamen and his queen had been found in the Valley of the Kings. He was convinced there were more artifacts and maybe even a tomb there. By 1909, with Carnarvon's backing, Carter was busy excavating. He found a few more artifacts but no tomb. Then World War I erupted, and Carter had to stop digging.

After the war, in 1917, Carter was back at it. This time he decided to dig systematically all around the Valley of the Kings. Five years later, he still hadn't found a tomb. Carnarvon was ready to give up. Carter asked him to fund one last dig. Carnarvon agreed.

As workers removed huts, rocks and soil on that last dig, in early November 1922, they noticed a step. Soon more steps came into view. They had found a stairway — and the top of a sealed door.

1922 Banting develops insulin

When he was a young teen, Frederick Banting's best friend died of diabetes. Banting was devasteted. The disease had left her unable to digest important nutrients in food. Banting became a doctor. While working at the University of Toronto in 1920, he decided to study diabetes.

Back in 1869, German medical student Paul Langerhans had discovered that special cells in the pancreas, a gland near the stomach, seemed to have something to do with digesting food. Twenty years later, doctors realized that those cells, called the islets of Langerhans, were linked to diabetes. Scientists began trying to isolate and extract whatever it was that the islets were producing, a hormone we now call insulin.

Banting and his team of Charles Best and James Collip worked with diabetic dogs, giving them the chemical they extracted from the islets. It took a lot of experiments, but eventually the team was successful — they were able to keep a diabetic dog alive using insulin. But would it work on humans?

In 1922, a 14-year-old boy dying of diabetes became the first human to receive insulin. His recovery was incredible. Insulin isn't a cure, but it helps control diabetes. Banting's discovery has saved the lives of millions.

Excited, Carter telegrammed Carnarvon: "At last have made wonderful discovery in valley; a magnificent tomb with seals intact; recovered same for your arrival; congratulations." On November 24, as Carnarvon waited anxiously, Carter made a small hole in the door and peeked in. And there it was — a tomb full of "wonderful things," as Carter later described it.

They widened the opening and entered the tomb. Inside they found jewelry, couches, vases, chariots and statues. Over the next two years Carter and his team discovered more rooms including the burial chamber of the young Tutankhamen — the best-preserved royal tomb ever found.

RIPPLES

Carter's find generated worldwide publicity and ignited "Tut mania." People everywhere were intrigued by the ancient pharaoh and Egyptian history. That fascination continues to this day.

1927 Robot revolution begins

The word "robot" was first used in 1921 in a stage play, but the first really useful robot wasn't invented until 1927. Televox, built by American engineer Roy Wensley, had a cardboard body and head. It could turn lights on and off, open windows, close doors on command and much more. But Televox was very primitive compared to today's robots. It couldn't roll around — it could only move its arms a little.

1928 Fleming develops penicillin

Oh, no! When Scottish scientist Alexander Fleming entered his lab in London, England, on September 3, 1928, he found that one of the samples of bacteria he was growing had been left open. Fleming was already known as a brilliant — but messy — researcher.

Mold had dropped on a bacteria sample, contaminating it. Now Fleming would have to start all over. But before throwing out the spoiled experiment, he took a quick look at it — and discovered something amazing.

Where the mold had landed on the sample, the bacteria around it had been destroyed. Fleming grew a sample of the mold and found it released a bacteria-killing substance. At first he called it "mold juice," but after a few months, he renamed it penicillin.

Fleming had worked in battlefield hospitals in France during World War I (page 76). He'd seen many soldiers die from infected wounds and knew how helpful a bacteria-killing drug could be. However, penicillin was difficult to isolate, and Fleming didn't think it would live long enough in the human body to kill disease-causing bacteria. After just a few years, he stopped studying it.

Then, in 1930, a doctor cured a patient with penicillin. By the early 1940s, scientists were able to concentrate penicillin and soon figured out how to mass-produce it to make it widely available.

RIPPLES

Penicillin was one of the first antibiotics ever discovered, and it changed medicine. Doctors used it to treat diseases that had infected people for thousands of years, including gangrene (death of tissue due to poor circulation) and tuberculosis (a lung disease). Soon scientists were searching for similar drugs that could treat other infections.

Fleming's discovery led to today's huge drug industry, and we're now able to make synthetic penicillin. Experts estimate that antibiotics have saved more than 200 million lives.

A robot is an intelligent machine that can perform jobs on its own or with guidance. It's usually guided by computer and electronic programming. Greek and Chinese engineers began trying to build robots more than 2200 years ago. They constructed mechanical birds and figures powered by steam or air pressure.

Around 1820, Japanese inventor Tanaka Hisashige built incredibly complex mechanical toys that could do tasks, such as serving tea. But Televox could do much more than any of these machines.

RIPPLES

Since Televox, robots have relieved people of many repetitive, dangerous tasks, such as assembly-line work, sorting and heavy lifting. As well, robots can go places humans can't — to Mars, into a volcano or deep down in the ocean. Bomb disposal squads use robots instead of endangering human beings. Robots can also help people with physical disabilities. As the world's population gets older, there will be more and more uses for robots.

Science fiction stories sometimes tell of robots running amok, destroying everyone and everything in their paths. That led science fiction writer Isaac Asimov to come up with his three laws for robots:
1. A robot may not injure a human being or, through inaction, allow a human being to come to harm.
2. A robot must obey the orders given it by human beings, except where such orders would conflict with the First Law.
3. A robot must protect its own existence as long as such protection does not conflict with the First or Second Law.

1929 Wall Street crashes

Buy now! Pay later! Get rich quick! For almost a decade in the 1920s these words echoed through New York's Wall Street, America's financial center, and caused many to rush to buy stocks with little cash. (A stock is a tiny share in a business.) Then during the fall of 1929, Wall Street crashed.

Stocks were now worthless. Ordinary people lost their jobs and homes. America was plunged into what became known as the Great Depression, which soon became a worldwide depression. Some analysts say it wasn't until the end of World War II (page 86) that jobs became plentiful again.

1930 Building the Empire State Building

The Empire State Building in New York stands out as an engineering feat and an architectural gem. It all came about because of a race.

At the height of the Great Depression, car magnate Walter Chrysler decided to construct a skyscraper. John Jakob Raskob from rival General Motors vowed to build one even taller.

Crowds watched in awe as a huge hole was dug in 1930, and Raskob's Empire State Building rose floor by floor. Construction was completed under budget in just over 13 months.

Opening on May 1, 1931, the Empire State Building was the tallest skyscraper in New York until the World Trade Center was built in 1972. It continues to be a tourist attraction and a beloved symbol of the energy and drive of New York City.

1930 Gandhi's Salt March

The British had ruled India for about 80 years when salt became an issue. In a hot country such as India, salt is vital. It replaces minerals in the body lost while sweating, and everyone, especially farm laborers and others who do hard physical work, needs salt. But the British would not allow Indians to produce or sell salt themselves — it was illegal. To get salt they had to buy highly taxed British-produced salt, and the money went to support the British rule.

The Indian people grew increasingly angry. They wanted the tax abolished — and they also wanted their independence from England. Mahatma Gandhi, an Indian leader who practiced and preached *satyagraha* — nonviolent civil disobedience — led the Indian people in protesting the salt tax and in seeking independence.

In 1930, he sent a letter explaining his position to the English viceroy, Lord Irwin, but the viceroy ignored it.

So on March 12, Gandhi and a group of his followers began a 24-day trek to the sea. There, on April 5, Gandhi broke the law by making a lump of salt. His followers did the same. His nonviolent protest set off two months of further demonstrations. Thousands were arrested, including Ghandi himself.

RIPPLES

Gandhi continued to campaign for independence from Britain. India finally achieved its independence in 1947.

Gandhi was assassinated by an extremist in 1948. But his ideas about nonviolent protest live on and have inspired many leaders, including the American civil rights leader, Martin Luther King Jr. (page 97).

1933 Hitler seizes power in Germany

The early 1930s was a time of uncertainty and turmoil in Germany. The country was humiliated by its defeat in World War I (page 76) and struggling economically.

Germany was eager to find a way out of its problems and back to the glory of its past. Adolf Hitler, a former army corporal, and his National Socialist Party (Nazi Party) promised that and more. His book *Mein Kampf* ("*My Struggle*") outlined his beliefs that Aryan Germans (non-Jewish Caucasians usually having Nordic features) were superior to other people, especially Slavic, Black and Jewish people.

In 1930, Hitler denounced Germany's politicians for causing the country's defeat in World War I. He blamed Germany's economic problems on Jewish financiers and promised to return Germany to its former glory.

In 1932, the Nazis won the national election, and by January 1933, Hitler had become chancellor and head of the government. When the Reichstag, the German parliament, burned (probably the work of Nazis), Hitler used the opportunity to arrest his opponents and seize unlimited power.

RIPPLES

Hitler pursued his policy of territorial expansion by invading Poland in 1939. His actions led to World War II (page 86). During the war, Hitler followed through on his promise to create an Aryan nation, by murdering millions of Jews and other non-Aryans.

1936 Berlin Olympics and the Nazis

The 1936 Olympics were a perfect opportunity for Germany's Chancellor Adolf Hitler and his racist Nazi Party to flaunt their power and beliefs. They decided to use the games to show the world that they were truly Aryans, a master race, as their propaganda claimed. Their most famous athlete, Luz Long, looked the part. He was blond and blue-eyed, as well as an amazing long jumper.

But what were they going to do about Black-American runner Jesse Owens? What if he beat a Nazi athlete?

Owens not only won four gold medals at the Olympics but defeated Long in the long jump.

And Long was not only gracious in defeat but helped Owens prepare before the jump. The two men became friends. Owens said, "You can melt down all the medals and cups I have, and they wouldn't be a plating on the 24-karat friendship I felt for Luz Long at that moment …"

Despite the Nazis' Aryan propaganda, the games went smoothly, and Germany was complimented for its efficient Olympics. But tensions between Germany and other countries over territory were growing. Hitler's desire for Aryan supremacy and more German territory would lead to World War II (page 86).

1939 World War II

Twenty-one years after World War I (page 76), the world was plunged into another world war. Many historians believe that tensions started with the peace treaty that ended World War I.

That treaty forced Germany to pay large amounts of money to the victorious Allies (countries that had fought against the Germans, such as France and England). Limits were placed on the size of the German military, and Germany was stripped of its colonies. German resentment grew, and its new government faced political instability and an economic depression.

By 1933, Germany had embraced a new leader, Adolf Hitler, and his Nazi Party. Hitler wanted a country built on racial purity, strong central leadership, reoccupation of lost lands and a powerful military. He began by reestablishing military control over the Rhineland, which violated the peace treaty. Then his army marched into Austria and annexed it (took it over). Other nations tried to stop Hitler through diplomacy, but it did not work.

Hitler next invaded the Sudetenland, a region of Czechoslovakia with a large German-speaking population. In 1939, Hitler signed a nonaggression pact with Joseph Stalin in the Soviet Union, which meant the two countries would not attack one another. Then, on September 1, Germany invaded Poland. Britain and France reacted. Poland was their ally. Hitler had gone too far.

On September 3, 1939, France and Britain declared war on Germany. Britain's dominions (Australia, Canada, New Zealand and South Africa) followed its lead. But even this huge opposition didn't stop Hitler. In 1940, Germany invaded Denmark, Norway, the Netherlands, Luxembourg, Belgium and finally France.

Country after country fell to the Germans. Soon only England and its dominion forces were left to oppose Hitler. Italy, which was ruled by Benito Mussolini, sided with the Germans.

In June 1940, Germany unleashed a blitzkrieg

("lightning war") against Britain, bombing its cities from airplanes. Under the determined leadership of Prime Minister Winston Churchill, Britain withstood the Blitz, as it was called.

In late May 1940, Britain began to evacuate more than 300 000 trapped English, French and Belgian troops from the French port of Dunkirk. Although thousands died under intense gunfire from the Germans, the evacuation was a success and a boost to British and French morale. But their joy was brief as Hitler continued to conquer more countries. Yugoslavia and Greece fell, as did much of North Africa.

In June 1941, Hitler invaded the Soviet Union, ending his pact with that country.

Meanwhile, the Japanese were keen to expand their power in Asia and acquire new lands. In 1931, Japan invaded Manchuria and in 1937, China. The United States and Europe stopped all shipments of steel, oil and iron to Japan. In retaliation, Japan launched a surprise attack on the American naval base in Pearl Harbor, Hawaii, on December 7, 1941. The United States declared war on Japan. Germany, Japan's ally, declared war on the United States. The war expanded across the world.

In 1943, the tide began to turn in the Allies' favor. (The Allies now included many countries, including the Soviet Union and the United States.) There were American victories in the Pacific against Japan, German defeats in eastern Europe and an Allied invasion of Italy. In 1944, the Allies invaded and took back France, while the Soviets pushed the Germans out of Russia and invaded Germany.

On April 30, 1945, Hitler committed suicide. The German forces surrendered soon after. On May 8, 1945, Victory in Europe ("VE Day") was declared, ending the war in Europe.

But the fighting carried on in the Pacific. That spring and summer, the Americans defeated Japan in major battles, but Japan refused to surrender. To end the war, the United States dropped the first atomic bomb (page 89) on the Japanese city of Hiroshima. When that failed to bring about a surrender, they dropped a second bomb on the city of Nagasaki, altogether killing or injuring more than 200 000 people. Japan formally surrendered on September 2, 1945.

The terrible war that had engulfed the world for six years was finally over. It had decimated cities and towns, separated and destroyed families and caused people to flee their homes and communities. It had killed more than 50 million civilians and soldiers.

RIPPLES

Nazi war criminals were tried and convicted for the murder of millions of people, including six million Jews.

The United States helped Europe rebuild after the war by sending money and technical aid. It occupied Japan from 1945 to 1952.

The Allies formed the United Nations (page 90) in the hope that international disputes in the future could be settled peacefully.

1939 **First computer built**

Although Charles Babbage (page 57) had designed computer-like machines, none of his machines was ever completed in his lifetime. Most scientists agree that the first computer was built in 1939 by American inventors John Vincent Atanasoff and Clifford Berry. They called it the Atanasoff-Berry Computer, or ABC.

A computer is basically a machine that can be programmed to automatically speed through a sequence of mathematical or logical operations. The computer can be reprogrammed to run more than one kind of program, such as predicting the weather or counting votes.

The 1939 ABC computer couldn't be programmed, but it was a starting point. Scientists worked to improve the computer, concentrating on two areas: building a better machine (the hardware) and creating the programs (the software).

The ENIAC computer of 1946 is sometimes called the first programmable general-purpose digital electronic computer. Its improved hardware resulted in computing power 1000 times faster than other machines of the time.

On the software side, in 1948 scientists at the University of Manchester in England created the Manchester Small Scale Experimental Machine, or "Baby." It was the first computer that could store program instructions in its electronic memory. But it was an experimental computer, and by the next year, scientists had incorporated its parts into a larger machine, the Manchester Mark 1.

Early computers, including the ENIAC, were huge, some more than twice as big as a classroom. That's because they were powered by vacuum tubes, which were large glass tubes. The tubes also became very hot and were unreliable — there could be thousands of vacuum tubes in a computer, and if just one burned out, the whole computer would shut down.

When transistors (page 90) began replacing vacuum tubes in the late 1950s, computers became smaller, more powerful and more reliable. Putting hundreds of transistors on a tiny microchip (page 94) made computers even smaller — and millions to billions of times more powerful than the early computers.

RIPPLES

It's hard to imagine anything today that's not run or made by computers. These "mechanical brains" operate traffic signals and assembly lines, keep track of medical records, fly planes and much more. They are used to design cars, buildings and other machines, to create special effects in movies — the list goes on and on.

Computers made complicated calculations possible and solved many of the problems of space exploration. The computers first used for launching spacecraft filled huge rooms but had far less computing power than today's laptops.

And, of course, the computer has led to the Internet (page 100), personal computers (page 101) and the World Wide Web (page 107), as well as many other technologies — including video games. This was definitely an invention calculated to change the world!

1939 Nuclear fission discovered

The process of nuclear fission was discovered in 1939 by German chemists Otto Hahn and Fritz Strassmann, and Lise Meitner, a physicist from Austria. They knew about the work of Niels Bohr (page 75) and Ernest Rutherford (page 79) and the structure of atoms. Hahn and Meitner experimented with bombarding atoms of uranium, a radioactive substance, with neutrons (small particles found in the nucleus, or center, of an atom).

The process they discovered was nuclear fission. During this process, an atom's nucleus splits into tinier particles. Small particles called neutrons and photons are produced, and so is a huge amount of energy.

Scientists soon realized that nuclear fission could create energy for nuclear power — but it could also power nuclear weapons. In fact, nuclear fission was the energy behind the nuclear, or atomic, bomb that ended World War II (page 86).

Today, nuclear fission makes up about 17 percent of the world's power supply. That will increase as more nuclear plants come into use. A nuclear reactor plant can produce power for 20 years without refueling. But nuclear power can also result in disasters such as the nuclear accident in Chernobyl, Ukraine (page 104).

1945 Atomic bomb is dropped

By the summer of 1945, World War II (page 86) had ended in Europe, but the war with Japan raged on. U.S. president Harry Truman wanted to end the war.

The United States had a secret weapon, the hugely destructive atomic bomb, which he hoped would show the Japanese that they were overpowered and force them to surrender.

On August 6, the first-ever atomic bomb was dropped on the Japanese city of Hiroshima. The result was a devastating explosion. Some 66 000 people died, and 69 000 were injured, but Japan did not surrender.

On August 9, another bomb was dropped on Nagasaki. Half the city was leveled, and thousands were killed or injured. On September 2, 1945, Japan formally surrendered.

RIPPLES

Aside from the immediate loss of life, radiation poison eventually killed more people in Japan. Future generations may also have suffered increased health problems, such as leukemia, passed on by parents who were exposed to radiation.

Hiroshima and Nagasaki showed the world the dramatic and horrific results of using atomic weapons. It ended World War II, but in the following years more countries developed their own atomic bombs and sometimes brought the world to the brink of nuclear war. Nations continue to struggle with the use and control of these deadly weapons.

1945 United Nations established

World War II (page 86) destroyed the lives of millions of people. The leaders of the "Big Four" countries (the United States, Britain, the Soviet Union and China) knew they had to find a way to prevent another world war and reduce world conflicts. In 1944, delegations from the Big Four met at a mansion called Dumbarton Oaks in Washington, D.C., to discuss the establishment of an international organization. Its aim would be to foster world peace, justice, human dignity and fairness. It would be called the United Nations (UN).

The League of Nations, established after World War I (page 76), had had similar goals, but it failed to keep the peace. Perhaps that was because not all of the major powers supported the League, and some, such as the United States, never joined. Other countries, including Japan and the Soviet Union, were no longer members by the 1930s. But now, at the end of this second terrible world war, it was clear that the world needed to work toward peace again.

On October 24, 1945, the UN Charter was ratified. The UN was officially born.

RIPPLES

Since 1949, the UN has been headquartered in New York City, but its land and buildings are considered international territory.

All of its members have one vote in the General Assembly. The Assembly's main role is to discuss issues, set standards and help establish international law. The UN's 15-member Security Council is responsible for international peace and security.

Today, the UN has more than 190 member countries. Over the years, the UN's work has branched out into human rights, emergency aid, economic development and international law, but its primary focus remains world peace.

1947 Transistor invented

When American physicists John Bardeen, William Shockley and Walter Brattain created the transistor in December 1947, no one was excited. But soon scientists were saying the transistor was the 20th century's greatest invention.

Before the transistor, devices such as televisions, radios and computers were powered by vacuum tubes. Transistors are much smaller and lighter than vacuum tubes. They're also cheaper to make and more reliable. Transistors became the basis of almost all modern electronic devices.

Computers, calculators, telephones, televisions — all became smaller and more powerful with transistors. But transistors would really change the world when they became part of microchips (page 94).

1948 Creation of the State of Israel

For centuries, Jews, Muslims and Christians have had strong religious ties to a small area in the Middle East that some call Palestine and others call Israel. After the murder of six million Jews in Europe by Hitler's Nazi regime during World War II (page 86), there was a renewed drive to create a Jewish state in the area then under British control. It would be the world's first Jewish state in 2000 years. As the Jewish campaign to establish a state intensified and opposition increased from the large local Arab population, the British, who had ruled Palestine since 1923, withdrew.

On November 29, 1947, the United Nations General Assembly voted to divide Palestine into Jewish and Arab sectors. The State of Israel was born in 1948 to rejoicing among Jews around the world and anger among Arab people. Arab countries including Jordan, Egypt, Syria, Iraq and Lebanon immediately declared war on the new State of Israel.

RIPPLES

Mistrust, conflict and tension have continued between Israel and its Arab neighbors, resulting in full-scale wars in 1948, 1967 and 1973 and smaller conflicts in 1982 and 2006. Despite attempts at peace negotiations, the disputed issues of land and borders have not been resolved.

1949 People's Republic of China established

It cost many lives and devastated a huge country. From the 1920s until 1949, the Chinese Communist Party, led by Mao Zedong, and the Kuomintang (KMT, or Chinese National People's Party), led by Chiang Kai-shek, fought for control of China. The civil war was interrupted for a few years when the Japanese threatened to invade all of China in 1931. It resumed in 1945 after World War II (page 86).

The Communists had a strong, disciplined organization and many weapons, acquired after the Japanese were ousted from Chinese territory. They promised land to peasants who'd been kept poor by rich landlords. The Nationalists were plagued by corruption and mismanagement.

After a series of military victories, in 1949 the Communists triumphed and declared the establishment of the People's Republic of China. The Nationalists were forced into exile on Taiwan, a large island off of China.

RIPPLES

For many years after the end of the civil war, the Chinese people faced difficult economic conditions and political repression. With the establishment of a market-based economy in 1978, China has prospered and opened up contact with the West. China is still ruled by a single political party, the Communist Party, which maintains strict control over life in the country.

1953 DNA molecule unraveled

For a long time, people had been interested in how organisms pass on their characteristics. How, for example, does a kitten inherit its coloring from its parents? Then, in 1866, Gregor Mendel proved with his pea experiments that traits are passed on in packages we now call genes (page 64).

Since then, scientists have learned that genes are part of DNA (deoxyribonucleic acid), which is in every cell in your body. DNA is like a recipe — it contains the instructions needed for the development and functioning of living organisms, and it allows a plant or animal to pass along characteristics to the next generation.

Science took a big step forward in 1953 when biologists James Watson (an American) and Francis Crick of England figured out that the DNA molecule looked like a twisted ladder, or, as scientists say, a double helix.

The discovery of DNA's double helix structure was the first big step in helping scientists understand DNA better. Gradually, they learned how DNA is stored and copied.

Today, scientists are already modifying genes in food crops to resist diseases and for other purposes. In future, doctors may use gene therapy to alter human genes to get rid of diseases such as cancer.

1953 Hillary and Norgay climb Mount Everest

Edmund Hillary, a New Zealand beekeeper, was passionate about climbing mountains. Tenzing Norgay, a skilled Sherpa guide from Nepal, had helped lead many climbing expeditions.

Both men were determined to reach the top of Everest, the highest mountain in the world. Avalanches, crevasses, sudden storms, intense winds, freezing temperatures and the extreme fatigue, headaches and nausea of oxygen depletion at high altitudes made climbing Everest dangerous.

Many expeditions had already tried and failed. Some climbers, such as George Mallory and Andrew Irvine in 1924, had even perished in the attempt. But Hillary and Norgay were determined. In the spring of 1953, they joined an expedition to summit Everest. Although the brutal conditions forced many to turn back, Hillary and Norgay continued up the mountain. On May 29, 1953, they reached their goal — the summit of Everest!

In the years that followed, Hillary continued to climb and also explored the Antarctic and the South Pole. He helped the Nepalese people build hospitals and schools and worked toward designating the Nepalese mountains as a national park.

Norgay trained South Asian boys and girls in mountaineering and provided scholarships for their education. Although Norgay himself never learned to read, he spoke several languages and dictated several books about Everest and mountaineering.

1955 Salk develops polio vaccine

When a vaccine for polio was announced on April 12, 1955, there were celebrations around the world. Other diseases were more devastating, but polio especially affected children, killing them or leaving them paralyzed.

Polio is short for poliomyelitis, also known as infantile paralysis. It has infected people for thousands of years — there are ancient Egyptian paintings showing people with the disease. People were terrified of polio, and it was one of the most dreaded diseases of children in the 1900s. Even today, there is no cure for it.

Dr. Jonas Salk was an American medical researcher who began working on polio with a research team in 1948. It took them seven years to develop a vaccine, but what a change they made. At its worst, polio paralyzed or killed up to 500 000 people every year around the world. Probably one of the most famous people with polio was U.S. president Franklin D. Roosevelt.

Thanks to Dr. Salk's vaccine, North America was declared polio free in 1994. The disease now exists in only a few countries, with fewer than 2000 cases reported around the world each year.

1957 First satellite launched

The Space Age started October 4, 1957, when Russia launched the satellite *Sputnik 1*. A satellite is anything that orbits a planet. For instance, the Moon is a satellite of the Earth. But *Sputnik 1* was the first artificial satellite to orbit the Earth — its name is Russian for "traveling companion."

Sputnik 1 was a metal sphere about the size of a beach ball, with four antennae, each approximately 2.6 m (8.5 ft.) long. It could transmit radio signals back to Earth.

On December 19, 1958, the United States launched Project SCORE (Signal Communication by Orbiting Relay Equipment), the world's first communications satellite. Probably the most important thing communications satellites have done is make international phone calls — especially in remote areas — possible and inexpensive.

Satellite technology evolved a lot in the next decades and changed how people communicated. It also changed how TV and radio were broadcast and much more. Satellites are used in weather forecasting, videoconferencing, long-distance learning, navigation and military applications. People in remote areas rely on satellites for their Internet connections.

Space exploration satellites, or space probes, send back detailed images and other information about space. The data they've sent back have led to many important discoveries, including the rings of Jupiter.

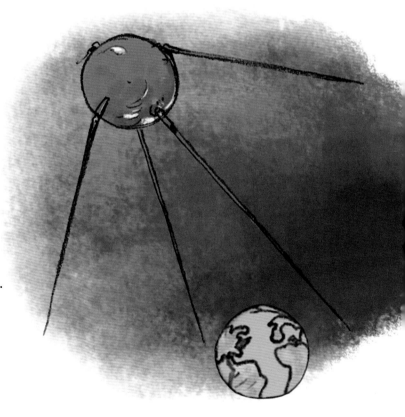

1958 Kilby invents microchip

After the transistor was invented in 1947 (page 90), scientists realized that if one transistor was good, then several connected together on a unit would be better (more powerful). On September 12, 1958, American physicist Jack Kilby demonstrated the integrated circuit, also called the chip or microchip. It had just a few transistors. Today billions of transistors can be placed on one microchip.

Microchips are cheap and tiny. They led to less expensive, smaller, more powerful computers.

The microchip started a computer revolution. Many inventions depend on the microchip, including cars, space probes and cell phones. Today, almost anything that uses electricity contains a microchip.

1959 Leakey discovers ancient skull

The place: sun-baked Olduvai Gorge, eastern Africa. The date: July 17, 1959. British archaeologist Mary Leakey noticed a piece of bone she thought might be part of an ancient human skull.

When Leakey and her team excavated the skull, they knew they had found something incredible. The skull was 1.7 million years old. It was older than any skull found up to that point and showed that human-like beings had been around much longer than anyone had considered possible.

Older skulls have since been discovered, but Leakey's find changed people's understanding of human evolution.

1960 First woman prime minister

Sirimavo Bandaranaike rose to power in Ceylon (now Sri Lanka) after her husband's assassination. He had been prime minister, and she took over from him, becoming the world's first woman prime minister. She held the post three times and was active in public life for more than 40 years. Her daughter, Chandrika Kumaratunga, served as president and prime minister of Sri Lanka after her.

In 1966, Indira Gandhi of India became the world's second woman prime minister, and in 1969, Golda Meir of Israel became the third. Since then, women have continued to hold leadership roles in countries around the world.

In 2012, there were 18 women prime ministers or presidents.

1960 Maiman invents laser

When the laser was first demonstrated by Theodore H. Maiman, an American physicist, on May 16, 1960, no one knew how to make use of it.

The first widespread use of lasers was in 1974, with barcode scanners. Now people use lasers daily in printers and CD and DVD players, to transmit phone calls and e-mails, for surgery and more.

The word "laser" stands for Light Amplification by the Stimulated Emission of Radiation. A laser is a very focused beam of colored light.

1961 Berlin Wall separates a city

In the darkness of the early morning of August 13, 1961, the Soviet-controlled East German government began to build a wall through the city of Berlin. A cinder-block and barbed-wire wall with watchtowers was quickly constructed, dividing the city in two. (Later, a more foreboding concrete wall was built.) Guard dogs and well-armed men patrolled the wall to prevent East Germans from entering West Berlin.

East Germans had been fleeing across the border to West Berlin since the end of World War II, hoping for better economic opportunity and greater political freedom. The Berlin Wall stopped that. It also separated families and increased tensions between East and West.

In the early years of the wall, it's estimated that about 5000 people managed to escape from East Germany to the West. Security tightened in the 1970s and 1980s, and it became increasingly difficult to get out. Some people still tried, and almost 200 died in the attempt.

RIPPLES

In the late 1980s, Communist governments in eastern Europe began to collapse (page 105). Country after country began to turn from communism. In November 1989, the East German government relented and opened the wall. East and West Berlin were reunited. In October 1990, Germany as a whole was reunited and became one country again.

ca 1962 Beatles revolutionize music

Paul McCartney, John Lennon, George Harrison and Ringo Starr — they called themselves the Beatles, and their music launched a passionate, worldwide following known as Beatlemania. From the early 1960s on, the "Fab Four" from Liverpool, England, revolutionized the music industry. They wrote and performed material that combined different musical styles, such as rock and roll, classical and pop ballads. They made promo films that led to the creation of the music video. Their hairstyles, clothing and attitude inspired a whole generation. The band broke up in 1970 but has continued to influence countless musicians around the world. They remain one of the bestselling groups in the history of popular music.

1962 *Silent Spring* warns of environmental danger

"Sinister" and "hysterical" were just two of the insults hurled at Rachel Carson's 1962 book *Silent Spring*. But Carson was not deterred by the attempts to silence her protests. She refused to give up the fight to preserve the natural world from the ravages of pesticides, which were killing insects, birds and animals. The oceans and lands were too precious.

Growing up on a farm in rural Pennsylvania, Carson loved nature. She became a marine biologist and began to write articles and books about nature and the need to protect it. Her 1951 book *The Sea Around Us* was a bestseller and propelled her into the spotlight.

But it was *Silent Spring* and its exposure of the harmful effects of the pesticide DDT that catapulted her to fame and controversy.

RIPPLES

Silent Spring alerted the public to the dangers of pesticides and the damage we are doing to the natural world. It paved the way for the environmental movement that followed it.

1963 King's "I have a dream" speech

It was the last speech of the day during the March on Washington, a civil rights protest to end discrimination and inequality between Blacks and Whites. Baptist minister Reverend Martin Luther King Jr., one of the organizers of the civil rights movement, walked to the podium at the Lincoln Memorial in Washington, D.C. Thousands waited to hear his words. TV cameras were poised to record the speech. From the first moment that Dr. King spoke, his eloquent words transfixed his audience.

His speech echoed the *Declaration of Independence*, that all men should be free. He declared his belief that the struggle for equality should be nonviolent.

RIPPLES

King's "I Have a Dream" speech mobilized people to push for civil rights and equality for Black people. It helped propel President Lyndon Johnson and the U.S. Congress to pass the 1964 *Civil Rights Act*. That same year, Dr. King won the Nobel Peace Prize. On April 4, 1968, as he was about to lead a protest march in sympathy with striking garbage workers in Tennessee, he was assassinated.

Some of his words that struck the strongest chord were, "I have a dream that one day this nation will rise up and live out the true meaning of its creed: 'We hold these truths to be self-evident — that all men are created equal.'"

1963 Kennedy assassinated

His assassination stunned the world. On November 22, 1963, as the dynamic 35th president of the United States, John F. Kennedy, waved to the crowds from a convertible slowly navigating the streets of Dallas, Texas, shots rang out. The president was hit. A few hours later, the youngest man ever elected president and the country's first Catholic president died. He'd been in office for only two years and ten months of a four-year term.

Lee Harvey Oswald was charged with killing the president but denied it. Two days later, while in police custody, Oswald himself was shot and killed by Jack Ruby.

RIPPLES

For years, the Kennedy assassination was investigated. Many theories arose about who shot Kennedy and why he was killed. Some believed Kennedy's murder involved several people. Others insisted it was the act of a single man.

After Kennedy's death, Vice President Lyndon Johnson became the 36th president of the United States. He continued many of Kennedy's policies, escalated U.S. participation in the Vietnam War and pushed through groundbreaking reforms in civil rights.

1969 Humans land on the Moon

On July 20, 1969, people sat glued to their TV sets as they watched a man in a bulky white suit, huge plastic helmet and giant boots step off the ladder of a spacecraft and onto the surface of the Moon. As he did so, U.S. astronaut Neil Armstrong said, "That's one small step for a man, one giant leap for mankind." Armstrong was the first person to set foot on the Moon, followed minutes later by fellow astronaut Edwin "Buzz" Aldrin. The two men spent the next two hours exploring the Moon's barren, rocky surface.

The American push to explore space and reach the Moon had begun in 1957 after the U.S.S.R. (Union of Soviet Socialist Republics, or Soviet Union) launched the first artificial satellite, *Sputnik 1*, into space (page 93). A month later, the Soviets sent a dog named Laika into space. Although Laika didn't survive, in 1961 the Soviets proceeded with the next and biggest step of all — sending an astronaut, Yuri Gagarin, into space.

The Americans worried that they were falling behind. In 1962, U.S. president John F. Kennedy urged NASA (National Aeronautics and Space Administration) to focus its attention on its Apollo Moon program. He vowed that the United States would put a man on the Moon before the Soviet Union did.

The space race was on! In the early 1960s, the Americans and Soviets sent more spacecraft into space. In 1966, the Soviet Union's unmanned *Luna 9* spacecraft landed on the Moon and sent back images. The race to land a man on the Moon heated up. It wasn't going to be easy or straightforward. There was much scientists didn't know about conditions on the Moon. Some were concerned that the Moon was covered with a thick blanket of dust that might engulf a spaceship. Geologists took Neil Armstrong and four other Apollo astronauts to the Grand Canyon to experience what they thought the Moon's surface might be like.

Just when it looked like the NASA space program was finally moving forward, a fire broke out on *Apollo 1* during a test launch on January 27, 1967. Three of the astronauts who had been scheduled to fly on the Moon mission were killed.

It was a terrible blow, and there was an immediate investigation, which recommended changes to future spacecraft. The Apollo Moon program got back on track. By 1969, astronauts Neil Armstrong, Buzz Aldrin and Michael Collins were getting ready to lift off.

On July 16, 1969, *Apollo 11* was launched from Florida with a manned module dubbed *Columbia* and a lunar lander, *Eagle*. For the next three days, *Apollo 11* and its astronauts headed toward the Moon.

When they finally walked on the Moon, Armstrong and Aldrin collected rocks and planted the U.S. flag. Then they headed home to a hero's welcome.

RIPPLES

Throughout the 1970s, the United States and the Soviet Union continued to send manned and unmanned spacecraft into space.

Soon, not just the Moon but other planets became the focus of their attention. In 1970, the Soviet Union's unmanned *Venera 7* landed on Venus. In 1971, their unmanned *Mars 3* probe touched down on Mars but failed after 20 seconds. In 1975, NASA's *Viking 1* successfully landed on Mars. It sent back the first photos and analyzed soil samples.

In the 1970s, as political tensions eased between the United States and the Soviet Union, the two countries embarked on joint space ventures, including launching the International Space Station, which began construction in 1998. Space telescopes and more satellites were also sent up. Other nations, including France, Canada, China and India, got involved in space travel. With each new foray into space, scientists learned more about our planet, our neighbors in the solar system and more distant parts of the universe. But it was the amazing images of a man walking on the Moon that first captured the public's imagination.

Race to the Moon time line

October 1957:	First artificial satellite orbits Earth: *Sputnik 1* (U.S.S.R.)
November 1957:	First animal in space: dog, Laika (U.S.S.R.)
August 1959:	First photograph of Earth from space: (U.S.)
April 1961:	First person in space: Yuri Gagarin (U.S.S.R.)
June 1963:	First woman in space: Valentina Tereshkova (U.S.S.R.)
February 1966:	First unmanned spacecraft lands on the Moon and sends back photos: (U.S.S.R.)
July 1969:	First men on the Moon: Neil Armstrong and Edwin Aldrin (U.S.)

1969 Internet developed

The idea of a network of computers was the brainchild of American professor Joseph Carl Robnett Licklider. In the early 1960s, he had a vision of a computer network that would link the world.

Building on Licklider's idea was a communications network called ARPANET (Advanced Research Projects Agency Network). The United States Department of Defense funded the development of the network. The American military wanted to use it to send important information to different locations, to be stored there in case there was another world war.

On October 29, 1969, Charley Kline, an American computer programmer and student working on ARPANET, tried to connect his computer to another computer using the system. Both computers immediately crashed! But an hour later, the computers were working again, and Kline sent the first message over the network.

The Internet — short for "internetwork" — grew out of ARPANET. The Internet evolved into a worldwide data communications system that transmits data by breaking it down into small chunks, called packets. Using a technology known as packet

1971 Guillet invents biodegradable plastic

More than 200 million tons of plastic are manufactured each year around the world. As plastics began to pile up in dumps, scientists wondered what to do. In 1971, Canadian chemist James Guillet invented a plastic that would eventually decompose when left in sunlight.

Biodegradable plastics are expensive, so scientists keep trying to create cheaper ones. Some are made of vegetable products, such as hemp, mixed with the plastic — these are called bioplastics. Others contain tiny amounts of metals, which help them break down when exposed to sunlight and oxygen. Microbiodegradable plastics include an additive that makes them break down with the help of soil microorganisms.

1973 Cooper invents cell phone

On April 3, 1973, people were amazed when American engineer Martin Cooper made a phone call from a New York City sidewalk using a cell phone he had developed. It weighed about 0.9 kg (2 lb.) — almost as much as a liter (quart) of milk.

At first, you could only talk on cell phones. Then smartphones were launched in 1993. Now you can take photos, access the Internet, text message, play games, watch movies — the list goes on and on.

Today, there are more than 5 billion cell phones. They have been used to find survivors during natural disasters, provide banking services where banks are scarce and even organize protestors to start revolutions.

switching, many people could use the same linked network.

Scientists kept working to improve the Internet and gradually made it more accessible to users. Today, it's a network of networks, wired and wireless, linking more than a quarter of the Earth's population.

RIPPLES

The development of the World Wide Web (page 107) allowed pictures and sound to be shown, heard and exchanged over the Internet. Suddenly the Internet wasn't just for computer geeks, it was for everyone.

The Internet has changed the way people shop, bank, share information and entertain themselves (games, music, movies) and even how they express themselves (blogs).

1975 Personal computer invented

With the invention of the microchip (page 94), many electronic devices, including computers, became a lot smaller. Computers shrank further when the microprocessor was invented in 1971 and reduced the size of the computer's central processing unit (CPU). (The CPU is the computer's brain — it's the part of the computer that performs what the computer program tells it to do.) For the first time, computers became small enough for home use.

The term "personal computer" was first used in 1975 by Ed Roberts, an American engineer, when he invented the first commercially successful personal computer. Many early personal computers, including Roberts's, had to be built by the users themselves from kits they ordered by mail. They were popular, but mostly just among people who had a technical background.

Then companies began to manufacture computers, with each new model faster or better than the one before. The first portable personal computer was demonstrated in 1981. It weighed more than 10 kg (23 lb.) — as much as a large bag of potatoes — so wasn't very convenient. It looked like a keyboard with a tiny screen built in.

Now there are more than 1.5 billion personal computers worldwide, and experts estimate that number will double in just a few years. The dream of a computer in every home was once thought to be impossible, but it's quickly becoming a reality.

RIPPLES

Personal computers made computing power available not just to governments and big corporations but also to small businesses and individuals. Computer manufacturers began designing with these new buyers in mind. They made computers faster and more powerful, and Web designers began to create a blizzard of websites to provide entertainment, convenience and more.

Computers have come a long way. Now tablet computers are small enough to slip into your pocket, so you can stay connected no matter where you go.

1976 *Viking* spacecraft lands on Mars

Is there life on Mars? This question has intrigued people for centuries. In the 1960s and '70s, the Soviet Union tried to find out by sending several space probes to Mars. Most failed, and none sent back any information.

In 1975, the United States sent two *Viking* landers (landing vehicles) to Mars to look for signs of life. *Viking 1* successfully landed on Mars on July 20, 1976. *Viking 2* followed on September 3. The landers took more than 50 000 images, which revealed river valleys, mountains that

appeared eroded by rain, lake beds and other signs of water. But there was no water, at least not on the surface, and so no likelihood of life on Mars.

RIPPLES

Viking 1 and *2* changed how we think about Mars. Information they sent back suggested it might once have had water — and therefore possibly life. Subsequent explorations to Mars have shown more and more evidence of water (page 112), but so far, no life.

1977 *Star Wars* revolutionizes moviemaking

"Along time ago in a galaxy far, far away …" With those words, movies changed forever. The plot of *Star Wars* wasn't new. It was like an old-fashioned science fiction cliff-hanger, with corny characters and a ferocious battle between good and evil. But no one had ever seen such special effects. Spaceships docked on super-real space stations. Lightsabers thrummed and cut.

The company that the movie's writer and director, George Lucas, created to produce those computer-based special effects is still at the forefront of many cutting-edge technologies, including computer graphics. Lucas's company pioneered most of the technological advances you see in movies.

Star Wars changed moviemaking in other ways. It introduced the modern special-effects blockbuster, as well as movie trilogies. This film also proved you could have a big hit without famous actors.

The movie set box office records. That gave

movie-theater owners money to build more theaters, which led to today's multiplexes. Theaters needed movies to show on those screens, so new movie companies started up.

The influence of *Star Wars* continues. People have tried to invent cool things from the movie, such as hologram images and giant AT-AT robots.

1979 Iranian revolution

In December 1978, two million Iranians filled the streets of Tehran and demanded an end to the rule of the monarch, Shah Mohammad Reza Pahlavi. Three months later, an Islamic religious leader, Ayatollah Ruhollah Khomeini, took over the Iranian government.

The toppling of the shah (ruler) caught much of the world by surprise. In power since inheriting the throne from his father in 1941, he had allied with the West against the Communist Soviet Union during the Cold War, a time of tension between Western countries and Communist regimes. Although the shah's rule was all-powerful and corrupt, he also modernized the country. He gave women more rights, improved education and health care and granted the peasants the right to own land. Iran's vast reserves of oil helped pay for the modernizations.

Many Islamic religious leaders opposed the shah's policies, which they thought were too westernized. And wealthy landowners resented the shah granting land to the peasants. They wanted an end to the shah's rule. After strikes and demonstrations that paralyzed the country, the shah fled Iran in early 1979. By April 1979, the Iranians voted to become an Islamic Republic.

After the Iranian revolution, the shah's efforts at modernization were reversed. The new religion-based government became more suspicious and hostile toward the West and its ideas.

ca 1980 HIV/AIDS spreads

Few people had heard of HIV or AIDS before the 1980s. That all changed around 1982. People learned that an infection called HIV (human immunodeficiency virus) can lead to AIDS (acquired immune deficiency syndrome), a life-threatening illness that makes people vulnerable to infections and cancers.

Genetic researchers believe that HIV originated in west equatorial Africa and was passed from chimpanzees to humans during the late 19th or early 20th century. There are many theories as to why and how HIV/AIDS adapted from an animal disease into one affecting humans, but no one has the full answer yet.

RIPPLES

At first, many people died because there were no drugs available to combat HIV or AIDS. Today, there are effective drugs that reduce the impact of the disease, although the drugs are expensive and not affordable in poorer countries.

To date, more than 30 million people around the world have died of AIDS-related illnesses. In 2009, nine countries in Africa had more than one-tenth of their populations aged 15 to 49 infected with HIV. HIV/AIDS remains a major world health problem.

1986 Chernobyl nuclear reactor disaster

It was supposed to be a routine check and a chance to run a few tests to see if the Chernobyl nuclear plant in Ukraine (part of the Soviet Union) would function well during a power outage. But the test turned into a nightmare.

At the start of the test, the plant's operators began to turn off the safety mechanisms. The next day, April 26, 1986, the plant's power dropped suddenly. The operators frantically tried to compensate for the loss of power, but there was little they could do.

RIPPLES

Thirty-two people died immediately after the explosion. Many more continue to suffer from long-term radiation damage and its increased risk for cancer. Lives were disrupted when people couldn't return to their communities. Nuclear safety was reevaluated around the world. Concerns about safety resurfaced after the 2011 earthquake in Japan (page 115), when nuclear reactors there were heavily damaged.

The reactor exploded at 1:23 a.m., spewing deadly radioactive material into the air.

It took two days for the world to learn what happened. While they were trying to keep the disaster secret, the Soviets attempted to clean it up. Firefighters tried to put out the fires caused by the explosion. Despite their frantic efforts, the fires raged for two weeks. The nearby town of Pryp'yat was evacuated on April 27. By May 14, about 116 000 people who'd been living within a 30 km (18.5 mi.) radius of the disaster were evacuated, too.

1989 Oil spill in Alaska

More than 41 million liters (11 million gallons) of black, sticky oil spilled over 2100 km (1300 mi.) of Alaskan coastline when the tanker *Exxon Valdez* struck a reef in Prince William Sound on March 24, 1989.

This oil spill wasn't the largest ever — the Gulf of Mexico spill in 2010 was bigger (page 114) — but many people estimate it caused more damage to the environment than any other spill. Prince William Sound is very remote, so it took a long time to get cleanup workers and equipment there. And wind and currents quickly spread the oil over a huge area, making the cleanup even tougher.

When the oil mixed with water, it became "mousse." This substance was even stickier than oil and thickly coated the birds and other animals. Their fur and feathers no longer insulated them, and many animals died of the cold. Animals that ate

the oil were poisoned. The oil spill killed hundreds of thousands of seabirds, salmon, otters, harbor seals, bald eagles and orcas.

Significant amounts of oil remain in many areas of Prince William Sound. Fish and bird populations are still greatly reduced and will be for many years.

1989 Tiananmen Square protest

Since late April 1989, hundreds of thousands of Chinese, many of them students, had been peacefully protesting against their government in Tiananmen Square in the center of Beijing, China. On June 3, the government warned it would end the protest. Tanks rolled into the square, soldiers opened fire on the unarmed protesters and by the next morning the protest was over.

Hundreds of protesters were killed — some reports have put the number much higher — and many of the protest's leaders fled the country. The protest inspired people in eastern Europe and helped lead to the collapse of the Soviet Union.

1989 Communism in Europe collapses

In the mid-1980s, the Communist countries dominated by the Soviet Union began agitating for change. They wanted more freedom and independence from Soviet control.

Shipyard workers in Poland led by Lech Walesa (below) began the protests with a series of work stoppages and demands for reforms. Many of their leaders were sent to jail, but the drive for change only increased.

When Mikhail Gorbachev became president of the Soviet Union in 1985, the push for reform sped up. Gorbachev proclaimed *glasnost* — a more open system of government with more freedom of speech for Russia and the other countries in the Soviet Union.

In 1989, Poland held the first non-Communist election in a Soviet country since 1948. Soon after, East Germans rallied for a greater voice in their government. The Berlin Wall (page 95) that had once divided the city was taken down, ending Communist rule in East Germany. One by one, other Soviet-led countries followed with reforms and democratization. Communism collapsed all over Europe with little bloodshed.

Communist governments were no longer in control of countries in eastern Europe or the Soviet Union. The Soviet Union was officially dissolved in late December 1991, and the countries that had once been part of it became independent. Communist parties still have a voice in eastern Europe, but they are not the only voice.

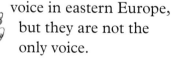

1990 Mandela is freed

Nelson Mandela is a Black South African leader who opposed the South African government's treatment of its Black citizens, especially its policy of apartheid. This policy kept Blacks separate from Whites and denied them political and economic opportunities. For example, Blacks and Whites could not marry or even live in the same part of town. Along with other political activists, Mandela led protests against the government's anti-Black policies.

For his protests, Mandela was sentenced in 1964 to life imprisonment. He spent 27 years in jail. His release in 1990 was applauded and celebrated around the world and signaled dramatic changes in South Africa.

RIPPLES

In June 1991, the South African parliament voted to repeal apartheid. In 1993, Mandela and Afrikaner leader F. W. de Klerk shared the Nobel Peace Prize for their efforts to change the apartheid system. The first multiracial national elections in South Africa were held in 1994, and Mandela became president of the country, the first Black person to do so. He held the office till 1999.

1990 Hubble Space Telescope launched

Hubble wasn't the first space telescope, but it's the best known because it has beamed back a huge amount of valuable data on the stars and planets. Pictures taken by telescopes on Earth can be distorted by the Earth's atmosphere. But Hubble orbits above the atmosphere, so its images are much clearer and therefore more useful to scientists.

How does Hubble gather information? As it travels through space, light from stars hits its main mirror, and then bounces onto another, smaller mirror. The second mirror focuses the light so it streams back through a hole in the main mirror, straight into Hubble's scientific instruments.

Hubble is about the size of a large school bus and is solar powered. It was launched by the space shuttle *Discovery* on April 24, 1990, and was designed to be serviced in space. So far, astronauts have gone on several service missions.

Hubble has led to many scientific breakthroughs, including the calculation of how fast the universe is expanding. It has also helped scientists estimate that the universe is 13 to 14 billion years old.

Want to see Hubble? Look online to find out when it will next be passing overhead in your area, then go out at night and take a look — Hubble will look like a fast-moving star.

1991 World Wide Web takes off

Tim Berners-Lee was frustrated. The British physicist and computer scientist was working at a physics lab in Geneva, Switzerland, with scientists from all over the world. They brought with them many types of computers. To get at the information on any of them, Berners-Lee had to log on to that computer. Sometimes he had to learn a new program first. Getting information was really difficult.

So Berners-Lee came up with the idea of a web of linked documents (Web pages) that could be accessed by any computer anywhere. The World Wide Web (WWW) launched on August 6, 1991. It provided a way of accessing information over the Internet through Web pages. People loved it. Within just five years there were 40 million users.

Berners-Lee invented three things that were crucial to the birth of the WWW. He developed uniform resource locators (URLs), which are like mailing addresses for sending information.

Then he created HyperText Markup Language (HTML). It's a code that a Web browser uses to show text and graphics. And Berners-Lee invented HyperText Transfer Protocol (HTTP), which lets people communicate using Web browsers and Web servers.

RIPPLES

Just think of all the ways you use the WWW daily to get information, stay in touch with friends, buy or trade things and much more. The WWW has also changed how quickly news spreads around the world and how people access entertainment, and it has created millions of jobs.

What does the WWW's inventor see in its future? Berners-Lee says, "The Web is a tool for communicating. With the Web, you can find out what other people mean. Let's use the Web to create neat, new, exciting things. Let's use the Web to help people understand each other."

1993 MP3s make music

The MP3 format for encoding and decoding music was first released in 1993, although it didn't get its name until 1995. Computers can rip, or import, audio files from CDs or collect them from other MP3 players. These files are easy to distribute to other users.

MP3s and similar formats have led to podcasts, audiobooks and portable music players that are incredibly small and lightweight. MP3 players can hold thousands of songs and have changed how people collect, listen to and share music. You can now listen to music on your cell phone, wristwatch — even your swim goggles!

1993 European Union comes together

The European Union (EU) was founded on November 1, 1993. But the idea for an association of countries from across Europe began after World War II (page 86) ended in 1945. Many of the countries' leaders wanted to do something to make sure war never happened again in Europe. So they began working toward an economic union that would bring the countries together.

In 1951, the European Coal and Steel Community united the six countries of Belgium, France, West Germany, Italy, Luxembourg and the Netherlands. Organizers thought that if countries traded with one another, they would be less likely to fight against each other again.

The European Coal and Steel Community and other similar organizations gradually evolved into the EU and added more members. Today, the EU is much more than a business association. The countries meet to decide on environmental policies, agriculture and development issues and more.

From Austria to the United Kingdom, there are more than 25 countries in the EU. The population of the EU is more than 500 million, and there are 23 official languages. The EU even has its own parliament, to which member countries send representatives.

Borders that once separated countries no longer do so. People in EU countries can go to school, live and work in another EU country as easily as in their home country.

Many countries in the EU use the euro for their currency, or money. Using just one currency makes trading easier. All euro coins have one side the same and the other side unique to each country. The paper money is identical throughout the EU.

1994 Chunnel rail tunnel opens

When the idea of a transportation tunnel under the English Channel connecting England and France was suggested in 1802, Britain wasn't interested. The Channel acted like a moat around Britain, making it difficult for enemies to attack.

But by the mid-1900s, a water barrier was no longer a great defense — airplanes had changed that. So construction of the Channel Tunnel began from England in 1987 and from France in 1988. In 1990 the tunnelers met.

The Chunnel is made up of three tunnels — two for passenger and freight trains and a third for service and security. Its undersea portion is the longest in the world.

1996 First mammal cloned

Her name was Dolly, and although she looked like an ordinary sheep, she became one of the most famous animals ever. That's because when Dolly was born on July 5, 1996, near Edinburgh, Scotland, she was the first mammal to be cloned from an adult animal.

A clone is a living thing derived from another living thing. As a result, the two have identical sets of genes. Clones are common in nature. For example, identical twins are clones because they have the same genes. Some forests originate from the sprouting roots of just one tree, so the trees are clones, too.

But Dolly was special. She was the result of cloning done deliberately by people. Also, scientists used cells from an adult animal to create her — Dolly was much younger than the sheep from which she was cloned, while identical twins are the same age.

Dolly wasn't the first animal to be cloned — that was a tadpole, back in 1952. And the tadpole had been cloned not from an adult cell but from an embryonic cell, or a cell in its earliest stages.

Some scientists believe that when a cloned animal is born, its body is actually the same genetic age as the animal it was cloned from. They think cloned animals therefore have shortened life spans, but other scientists disagree. Dolly the sheep died when she was just 6 years old, while other sheep of her breed tend to live to be 11 or 12 years old.

RIPPLES

Since Dolly was cloned, scientists have cloned a number of animals, including a cat, dog, horse and even an endangered animal, the gaur. In 2009, a Pyrenean ibex became the first extinct animal to be cloned. It was cloned from a frozen skin sample of an ibex, but died just minutes after it was born.

Many cloned animals are unhealthy and die of infections. And no one knows how cloning affects an animal's intelligence or personality. Because there is so much to learn about cloning, most scientists do not think humans should be cloned. What do you think about cloning humans?

1997 First Harry Potter book

Who could have guessed that J. K. Rowling's first book, *Harry Potter and the Philosopher's Stone* (or *Sorcerer's Stone* in America), would shoot to the top of the bestseller list? It was the first of seven books in a series that has sold more than 450 million copies, been translated into more than 65 languages and spawned several hit movies.

Some people believe that more kids are reading because of the popularity of the books. Many booksellers, authors and librarians feel there's been a surge of interest in fantasy books since the Harry Potter books were published.

2001 Terrorists attack World Trade Center and Pentagon

It was a bright, sunny September morning in New York when 19 hijackers took control of four commercial airliners over the United States. The planes were heavily fueled for the long flights they were about to make.

At 8:46 a.m., American Airlines flight 11 crashed into the World Trade Center's North Tower. Minutes later, a second plane hit the South Tower. Other hijackers flew American Airlines flight 77 into the Pentagon in Washington, D.C., at 9:37 a.m., and a fourth flight, United Airlines 93, which was probably headed for the Capitol or White House, was diverted by courageous passengers and crashed near Shanksville, Pennsylvania, at 10:03 a.m.

The two World Trade Center towers collapsed in the attack. Many nearby buildings were heavily damaged or destroyed. More than 3000 people were killed. Rescue personnel rushed in from around the city, risking their lives to evacuate buildings and help survivors reach safety. More than 400 were killed. It was soon clear that Osama bin Laden and his terrorist group, al-Qaeda, who lived in hiding in Afghanistan, had carefully planned and executed the attacks. Bin Laden's stated motives for the attacks were his opposition to the U.S. presence in Arab lands and the U.S. support of Israel.

2003 Social networking takes off

Keeping in touch with friends around the world became much easier in 2003 when Myspace was set up in Santa Monica, California. Facebook, a similar online social networking system, was launched in 2004 and by 2011 had more than 1 billion active users. Google+ attracted 25 million users in its first month in 2011.

Social networks let you communicate with friends and share photos, music, videos and more. With Twitter, you can "tweet" a message of up to 140 characters. Twitter has more than 200 million users. Many tweets are just between friends or from celebrities to their followers, but other tweets are sent by people witnessing, and reporting on, earthshaking events.

2003 Space Shuttle *Columbia* explodes

As it was about to land after a 16-day research flight, the space shuttle *Columbia* exploded, killing all seven astronauts. It was the 113th mission of the space shuttle program and *Columbia*'s 28th trip into space. The shuttle broke apart over Texas, scattering debris and shocking a nation.

An observer, Benjamin Laster of Kemp, Texas, recounted, "The barn started

shaking, and we ran out and started looking around. I saw a puff of vapor and smoke and saw big chunks of metal fall."

The cause of the explosion turned out to be a piece of insulating foam on the fuel tank that had fallen off and hit a wing. There was no time for the crew to do anything to prevent the explosion.

2003 Heat wave in Europe

Week after week, in the summer of 2003, the sun beat down on western Europe, causing heat waves, drought, forest fires — and more than 35 000 deaths. It was the hottest summer in Europe in almost 500 years, and high temperature records were shattered in many countries.

In Germany, rivers dried up and shipping was brought to a standstill. In France, nuclear reactors, usually cooled by river water, couldn't get the water they needed — river levels dropped too low. The reactors had to be shut down.

Between June and August 2003, many crops were lost, especially in southern Europe. More than 25 000 forest fires burned. Portugal was especially hard hit.

Heat waves have never been considered a major hazard, like floods or earthquakes, but they're likely to increase in number and severity as Earth's climate warms. Experts predict heat-related deaths could double in less than 20 years.

August 2003 was the hottest August on record in the entire northern hemisphere (that includes North America). Experts believe the increase in temperature during the 20th century is likely the largest and most rapid in the past 1000 years. The average global temperature is rising, and scientists warn that the world must cut the greenhouse-gas emissions that cause global warming.

2008 Search for life on Mars

Are we alone in the universe? In 2008, the *Phoenix* Mars lander, launched by the United States, brought us closer to an answer when it detected water in a soil sample from the surface of Mars.

Scientists know that for life to exist, three basic things are needed: a source of energy (Earth uses the Sun), the building blocks of life (carbon, in our case) and water. Finding liquid water on Mars was a big step forward in the search for alien life.

Because Mars is one of the closest planets to Earth, scientists have been especially interested in exploring it. Beginning in 1960, Russia (then the Soviet Union) and the United States have attempted to send more than 40 missions to Mars. Many of these spacecraft, whether flyby space probes, craft orbiting the planet or those that landed on the surface, sent back useful data to help scientists analyze Mars.

RIPPLES

Finding evidence of liquid water in Mars's past makes scientists even more determined to continue their search for life there.

Could there be life somewhere beyond Mars? Experts carefully examine any meteorites that land on Earth for bacteria or other tiny organisms that could have come from some other planet. And they continue to look for water on planets and moons in our solar system.

Now they're also using space telescopes to search for life beyond our solar system. Some scientists think that Alpha Centauri, Earth's closest star system, may contain planets that can support life.

Between 2030 and 2035, the European Space Agency plans to land humans on Mars. What do you think they will find?

For instance, in 1976, the *Viking 1* and *Viking 2* spacecraft landed on Mars and sent back data showing evidence that there had once been water on the planet (page 102).

Where is that water now? Over millions of years, Mars became too cold and its atmosphere too thin for liquid water to last on its surface. Instead, the water vaporized. Only frozen water (ice) has been found at the planet's poles.

On August 6, 2012, NASA rover *Curiosity* landed in a crater on Mars. Its mission: to assess if the soil there has, or ever had, the right conditions to support life. *Curiosity*'s soil tests have already shown that long ago there was likely flowing water in the area.

In November 2012, the spacecraft *MESSENGER* confirmed the presence of ice on Mercury. Scientists eagerly await more results about Mars, Mercury and the other planets.

2008 Obama becomes president of the United States

Many thought it would never happen, but in 2008, the United States elected its first president of African-American descent, Barack Obama.

It wasn't the only first in Obama's life and career. He was the first Hawaiian to become president. He was the first Black American to become editor of the *Harvard Law Review*. He was also one of the first to use social networking intensely to reach supporters in his election campaign. Obama was re-elected president in 2012.

2010 Floods, earthquakes and more natural disasters

There were about 950 natural disasters in 2010, making it one of the worst years ever for such catastrophes. They ranged from weather-related emergencies such as heat waves and hurricanes to geological calamities, including avalanches and earthquakes.

The year's deadliest natural disaster was the earthquake that struck Port-au-Prince, Haiti, in January. It killed more than 220 000. A volcano eruption in Indonesia killed hundreds, while one in Iceland created an ash cloud that covered most of Europe.

Global warming caused deadly heat waves in Russia and Japan. The worst flooding ever in Pakistan's history hit July 26. More than 20 million people were affected. Flooding in China killed more than 3000.

2010 Icelandic volcano disrupts travel

In April 2010, a little-known volcano on Iceland called Eyjafjallajökull erupted, spewing volcanic ash and steam almost 11 km (7 mi.) into the air. The ash cloud, carried by the jet stream, wafted toward Europe. Airports all over Europe shut down. Flying through ash could cause engine trouble on aircraft and lead to disasters.

The cancellation of flights in Europe set off a chain reaction of flight disruptions around the world that lasted for six days in April and started up again in May. The volcano's eruption proved again how powerful natural events can affect the world.

2010 Oil spill in Gulf of Mexico

It was the world's worst ever spill of oil into ocean waters. The disaster began on April 20, 2010, when an explosion rocked the oil rig *Deepwater Horizon*, located in the Gulf of Mexico. Eleven men died, and two days later, the rig sank.

The blast caused an underwater oil well to erupt, spewing oil into the water. The oil spread quickly, helped by strong winds. It polluted the coastlines of Alabama, Florida, Louisiana and Mississippi. It ruined the fishing industry and killed animals. And it could continue to affect wildlife in the area for decades to come — investigators believe there are large amounts of oil below the water's surface that may harm marine life.

The oil kept gushing for almost three months. About 4.9 billion barrels of oil leaked into the Gulf of Mexico. The drilling was carried out by the oil company BP, so the disaster is often called the BP oil spill.

It took many desperate attempts before the leak was sealed on September 19, 2010.

The BP spill was the most terrible environmental disaster in the United States, releasing many times more oil than the *Exxon Valdez* spill (page 104).

2010 The Arab revolutions

Some call it the "Arab Spring," a time of revolt and change in the Arab world. It started in Tunisia, with just one man, Mohamed Bouazizi, a poor seller of fruits and vegetables. He was distraught at being constantly harassed by the police and set himself on fire in protest. His death ignited a storm of public anger at the government of longtime Tunisian president Zine al-Abidine Ben Ali. Within days of Bouazizi's death, the president was ousted as leader.

The Tunisian protests inspired similar demonstrations in Egypt in January 2011 and forced President Hosni Mubarak to leave office. Demonstrations broke out in other Arab countries such as Yemen, Bahrain, Libya and Syria. People were tired of living under repressive regimes that limited their freedom and rights. They were angry about tough economic conditions, corruption and high unemployment. They wanted change.

RIPPLES

Each of the countries caught up in the Arab Spring movement has a different history, and each is made up of different political and ethnic groups. How these interests and groups interact will determine the social, economic and political effects of the Arab Spring in the years to come.

2011 Japanese earthquake

Mid-afternoon on Friday, March 11, 2011, the earthquake hit. Its epicenter was in the Pacific Ocean off northern Japan, and it caused a deadly tsunami (an unusually huge sea wave or series of waves caused by a quake or underwater volcanic eruption). The Japanese tsunami wave was estimated to be taller than 23.5 m (77 ft.).

The tsunami drowned many people and swept away homes, cars and even planes at a nearby airport. More than 15 000 people died, with many thousands more injured or missing.

The earthquake damaged roads and railways, and fires destroyed many buildings. The disaster also affected nuclear power plants, releasing deadly radiation.

The effects of the earthquake were felt as far away as North America's west coast. Since the disaster, Japan has experienced thousands of aftershocks, and these could continue for years.

RIPPLES

After the disaster, radiation was found in food and water in Japan. That made people all over the world reconsider the safety of nuclear power.

The magnitude-9.0 earthquake was powerful enough to move Japan 4 m (13 ft.) closer to North America and shift Earth's axis. The speed of Earth's rotation increased, which shortened the length of a day by 1.8 microseconds. Obviously, most people will never notice this, but it affects how spacecraft are navigated.

20?? What's the next big deal?

Turn on the TV and you'll hear commentators, scientists, historians and economists speculate about the future. Will the stock market go up or down? Will the latest revolution succeed or fail? How will global warming affect us? What about the latest technological device — how will it change our lives?

No one knows for certain what will happen tomorrow, of course, but we can make some good guesses by looking at the past. We'll have to deal with a changing and unpredictable climate and find new sources of energy that don't deplete the planet. There are likely to be more upheavals and revolutions when people are not content with their lives. And there may be a struggle between rich and poor over resources.

Despite uncertainty about the future, the past can help us understand and find ways to cope with whatever events become — the next big deal.

Time line

Use this time line as a guide and overview as you take a walk through history.

Date	Inventions & discoveries	Science, Mathematics & Medicine	Arts, Architecture & Language	History, Politics & Religion
6 000 000 – 40 000 BCE	ca 400 000 BCE Fire discovered (p. 7)		ca 50 000 BCE Language developed (p. 8) ca 40 000 BCE First cave paintings (p. 8)	ca 6 000 000 BCE First humans appear (p. 6)
39 999 – 3500 BCE	ca 3500 BCE Wheel invented (p. 12) ca 3500 BCE Plow invented (p. 12) ca 3500 BCE Sail invented (p. 13)			ca 8000 BCE Humans begin farming (p. 9) ca 8000 BCE Last big Ice Age ends (p. 10) ca 7000 BCE First cities appear (p. 10) ca 3500 BCE Horses first ridden (p. 11)
3499 – 1000 BCE	ca 3200 BCE Water pump invented (p. 13)	ca 2000 BCE Concept of zero developed (p. 15)	ca 3200 BCE Written language developed (p. 14) ca 2560 BCE Great Pyramid of Giza built (p. 15) ca 1100 BCE Alphabet developed (p. 17)	ca 2200 BCE Rise of Greece (p. 16) ca 1500 BCE Iron Age begins (p. 17)
999 BCE – 1 CE	ca 250 BCE Compass invented (p. 21)	ca 400 BCE Hippocrates revolutionizes medicine (p. 20) ca 250 BCE Archimedes changes math and science (p. 21)		776 BCE First Olympic Games (p. 18) ca 753 BCE Founding of Rome (p. 18) ca 560 BCE Buddha is born (p. 19) ca 551 BCE Confucius is born (p. 19) 508 BCE First voting (p. 20) ca 221 BCE Great Wall of China built (p. 22) ca 100 BCE Silk Road flourishes (p. 23) ca 100 BCE Rise of the Roman Empire (p. 24) ca 5 BCE Jesus Christ is born (p. 25)

Date	Inventions & discoveries	Science, Mathematics & Medicine	Arts, Architecture & Language	History, Politics & Religion
1 CE – 1000	105 Cai Lun invents paper (p. 26) ca 500 Spinning wheel invented (p. 28)	ca 800 ibn Hayyan develops scientific method (p. 29)	ca 800 Printing invented (p. 29)	79 Mount Vesuvius erupts (p. 25) ca 250 Golden age of the Maya (p. 27) ca 570 Muhammad is born (p. 28) ca 800 Age of the Vikings (p. 30)
1001–1400	1044 Gunpowder invented (p. 32) ca 1277 Huygens invents mechanical clock (p. 35)	1286 Eyeglasses invented (p. 36)		1096 Crusades begin (p. 32) 1206 Genghis Khan rules Mongol Empire (p. 33) 1215 King John signs Magna Carta (p. 34) 1271 Marco Polo treks to China (p. 35) 1337 Hundred Years' War begins (p. 36) ca 1347 Black Death breaks out (p. 36) ca 1400 Renaissance begins (p. 37)
1401–1550	ca 1440 Gutenberg invents printing press (p. 38)	1543 Copernicus shows Earth orbits the Sun (p. 45)	1503 Da Vinci paints *Mona Lisa* (p. 41) 1508 Michelangelo paints Sistine Chapel ceiling (p. 41)	ca 1490 Aztec Empire at peak (p. 39) 1492 Columbus reaches the Americas (p. 40) 1497 Cabot reaches the "New World" (p. 40) 1510 African slaves first shipped to the Americas (p. 42) 1519 Magellan sets out to sail around the world (p. 43) 1519 Cortés meets the Aztecs (p. 43) 1520 Suleiman rules the Ottoman Empire (p. 44) 1526 Mughal Empire begins (p. 44)

Date	Inventions & discoveries	Science, Mathematics & Medicine	Arts, Architecture & Language	History, Politics & Religion
1551–1750		1600 Gilbert explains electricity and magnetism (p. 46) 1609 Kepler publishes his laws of planetary motion (p. 48) 1609 Galileo revolutionizes astronomy (p. 48) 1687 Newton "invents" physics (p. 49)	ca 1595 Shakespeare writes *Romeo and Juliet* (p. 45)	1607 Jamestown becomes first colony in America (p. 47) 1608 Champlain establishes permanent settlement in Canada (p. 47) ca 1690 Dodo becomes extinct (p. 49)
1751–1800	1776 Steam engine invented (p. 51) 1800 Volta invents electric battery (p. 56)	1751 Discovery of the commercial potential of rubber (p. 49) 1796 Jenner develops vaccines (p. 55)	1790 Mozart composes (p. 55)	1759 Defeat of the French in Canada (p. 50) 1768 Cook explores the Pacific Ocean (p. 50) 1776 American Revolution (p. 52) 1781 Industrial Revolution begins in England (p. 53) 1789 French Revolution (p. 54)
1801–1850	1809 Appert develops first canned food (p. 56) 1821 Faraday invents electric motor (p. 57) 1822 Babbage invents a computer (p. 57) 1824 Braille invented (p. 58) 1844 Morse demonstrates electric telegraph (p. 60)	1816 Laënnec invents stethoscope (p. 56) 1842 Synthetic fertilizer invented (p. 59)	1826 Niépce takes first photographs (p. 59)	1825 Stephenson builds first steam railway (p. 58)
1851–1900	1856 Bessemer makes steel cheaply (p. 61) 1859 Lenoir invents internal combustion engine (p. 63) 1876 Refrigerator invented (p. 65) 1876 Bell invents telephone (p. 66) 1880 Edison invents lightbulb (p. 67) 1885 Benz builds first car (p. 68) 1900 Television invented (p. 70)	1854 Nightingale revolutionizes nursing (p. 61) 1859 Darwin presents his theory of evolution (p. 62) ca 1862 Pasteur's experiments lead to pasteurization (p. 63) 1866 Mendel experiments with genes (p. 64) 1895 Röntgen discovers X-rays (p. 69) 1898 Curie discovers two new elements (p. 69)		1866 Transatlantic telegraph cable links continents (p. 64) 1869 Suez Canal completed (p. 65) 1878 Fleming establishes standard time zones (p. 67) 1893 Women get the vote (p. 68)

Date	Inventions & discoveries	Science, Mathematics & Medicine	Arts, Architecture & Language	History, Politics & Religion
1901–1925	1901 Marconi sends radio signal across Atlantic (p. 70) 1903 Wright brothers fly first airplane (p. 71) 1907 Baekeland invents plastic (p. 73) 1920 Carver revolutionizes agriculture (p. 80) 1922 King Tut's tomb discovered (p. 80)	1905 Einstein discovers $E=mc^2$ (p. 72) 1913 Bohr explains the atom (p. 75) 1917 Rutherford splits the atom (p. 79) 1918 Fatal flu kills millions (p. 79) 1922 Banting develops insulin (p. 81)	1911 Art goes abstract (p. 74)	1904 Digging the Panama Canal (p. 72) 1909 Peary reaches the North Pole (p. 74) 1912 *Titanic* sinks (p. 75) 1914 World War I (p. 76) 1917 Russian Revolution and rise of communism (p. 78)
1926–1950	1927 Robot revolution begins (p. 82) 1939 First computer built (p. 88) 1947 Transistor invented (p. 90)	1928 Fleming develops penicillin (p. 82) 1939 Nuclear fission discovered (p. 89)	1930 Building the Empire State Building (p. 83)	1929 Wall Street crashes (p. 83) 1930 Gandhi's Salt March (p. 84) 1933 Hitler seizes power in Germany (p. 85) 1936 Berlin Olympics and the Nazis (p. 85) 1939 World War II (p. 86) 1945 Atomic bomb is dropped (p. 89) 1945 United Nations established (p. 90) 1948 Creation of the State of Israel (p. 91) 1949 People's Republic of China established (p. 91)
1951–1980	1958 Kilby invents microchip (p. 94) 1959 Leakey discovers ancient skull (p. 94) 1960 Maiman invents Laser (p. 94) 1969 Internet developed (p. 100) 1971 Guillet invents biodegradable plastic (p. 100) 1973 Cooper invents cell phone (p. 100) 1975 Personal computer invented (p. 101)	1953 DNA molecule unraveled (p. 92) 1955 Salk develops polio vaccine (p. 93) 1957 First satellite launched (p. 93) 1962 *Silent Spring* warns of environmental danger (p. 96) ca 1980 HIV/AIDS spreads (p. 103)	ca 1962 Beatles revolutionize music (p. 96) 1977 *Star Wars* revolutionizes moviemaking (p. 102)	1953 Hillary and Norgay climb Mount Everest (p. 92) 1960 First woman prime minister (p. 94) 1961 Berlin Wall separates a city (p. 95) 1963 King's "I have a dream" speech (p. 97) 1963 Kennedy assassinated (p. 97) 1969 Humans land on the Moon (p. 98) 1976 *Viking* spacecraft lands on Mars (p. 102) 1979 Iranian revolution (p. 103)

Date	Inventions & discoveries	Science, Mathematics & Medicine	Arts, Architecture & Language	History, Politics & Religion
1981–2000	1990 Hubble Space Telescope launched (p. 106) 1991 World Wide Web takes off (p. 107)	1996 First mammal cloned (p. 109)	1993 MP3s make music (p. 107) 1997 First Harry Potter book (p. 109)	1986 Chernobyl nuclear reactor disaster (p. 104) 1989 Oil spill in Alaska (p. 104) 1989 Tiananmen Square protest (p. 105) 1989 Communism in Europe collapses (p. 105) 1990 Mandela is freed (p. 106) 1993 European Union comes together (p. 108) 1994 Chunnel rail tunnel opens (p. 108)
2001–2012	2003 Social networking takes off (p. 110)	2008 Search for life on Mars (p. 112)		2001 Terrorists attack World Trade Center and Pentagon (p. 110) 2003 Space Shuttle *Columbia* explodes (p. 111) 2003 Heat wave in Europe (p. 111) 2008 Obama becomes president of the United States (p. 113) 2010 Floods, earthquakes and more natural disasters (p. 113) 2010 Icelandic volcano disrupts travel (p. 113) 2010 Oil spill in Gulf of Mexico (p. 114) 2010 The Arab revolutions (p. 114) 2011 Japanese earthquake (p.115)

Index

9/11, 110

ABC (Atanasoff-Berry Computer), 88
Africa, 6, 42, 65, 94, 106
Age of Discovery, 13
agriculture, 9, 10, 27, 59, 80
AIDS (acquired immune deficiency syndrome), 103
airplanes, 63, 71, 108, 110, 113
Alaska, 104
Aldrin, Edwin "Buzz," 98, 99
alphabet, 14, 17
al-Abidine Ben Ali, Zine, 114
al-Qaeda, 110
American Civil War, 42, 65
American Revolution, 52
antibiotics, 82
apartheid, 106
Apollo program, 98, 99
Appert, Nicolas, 56
Arabs, 26, 33, 91, 110, 114
Arab Spring, 114
Archimedes, 13, 16, 21
Aristotle, 16
Armstrong, Neil, 98, 99
ARPANET (Advanced Research Projects Agency Network), 100
art, 37, 41, 59
    abstract, 59, 74
    cave, 7, 8
Asimov, Isaac, 83
assembly lines, 68, 83, 88
astronauts, 71, 98, 99, 106, 111
astronomers, 15, 27, 45, 48
astronomy, 45, 48
Atanasoff, John Vincent, 88
atomic bombs, 72, 79, 87, 89
atoms, 75, 79, 89
Aztecs, 39, 43

Babbage, Charles, 57, 88
Babur, 44
Babylonians, 15
Bacon, Francis, 37
bacteria, 36, 82, 112
Baekeland, Leo Hendrik, 73
Baird, John Logie, 70
Bakelite, 73
Bandaranaike, Sirimavo, 94
Banting, Frederick, 81
Bardeen, John, 90
batteries, electric, 56
BCE (before common era), 5
Beatles, 96
Bell, Alexander Graham, 60, 66
Benz, Karl, 68
Berlin, 85, 95, 105

Berners-Lee, Tim, 107
Berry, Clifford, 88
Bessemer, Henry, 61
Best, Charles, 81
Bible, 25, 38, 41, 45, 48
bin Laden, Osama, 110
bioplastics, 9, 100
Black Death, 23, 36, 38
Blacks, 42, 97, 106, 113
Bohr, Niels, 75, 89
Bolsheviks, 78
bombs, 72, 79, 83, 86, 87, 89
Bonaparte, Napoleon, 54, 56
books, 26, 29, 36, 38, 107, 109
Botticelli, Sandro, 37
Bouazizi, Mohamed, 114
Braille, Louis, 58
braille, 58
Brandenberger, Jacques E., 73
Brattain, Walter, 90
Britain, 50, 52, 84, 108. See also England
Bronze Age, 17
Brunelleschi, Filippo, 37
bubonic plague, 36
Buddha, 19
Buddhism, 19, 23
Buonarroti, Michelangelo, 37, 41

cable, transatlantic, 64–65
Cabot, John, 40
Caesar, Augustus, 24
Caesar, Julius, 24
Cai Lun, 26
Canada, 40, 47, 50
canned food, 56
cannons, 32, 36
cars, 46, 49, 56, 61, 63, 68, 88, 94
Carson, Rachel, 96
Carter, Howard, 80, 81
Carthaginians, 24
Carver, George Washington, 80
Catholic Church, 34, 37, 45, 48
cave art, 7, 8
caves, 7, 8, 9
CDs, 94, 107
CE (common era), 5
cellophane, 73
cell phones, 56, 66, 70, 94, 100
Chauvet, France, 8
Chernobyl, Ukraine, 89, 104
China, 19, 22, 23, 33, 35, 87, 91, 105
Chinese National People's Party, 91
Christianity, 23, 25, 32, 33, 91
Christ, Jesus, 5, 25

Chrysler, Walter, 83
Chunnel, 108
Churchill, Winston, 86
circuit, integrated, 94
cities, 10, 14, 68
civilization, 7, 9, 14, 16, 17, 24, 27, 33, 39
civil rights, 84, 97
climate, 6, 7, 10, 111
clocks, 12, 35
cloning, 64, 109
cloth, 26, 28, 53
coal, 51, 53, 58, 63, 76
Cold War, 103
Collins, Michael, 99
Collip, James, 81
Columbia (spacecraft), 111
Columbus, Christopher, 23, 31, 35, 40, 43, 46
communism, 78, 91, 95, 103, 105
compasses, 13, 21, 30, 46, 48
computers, 12, 17, 26, 35, 46, 57, 83, 88, 90, 94, 100, 101, 102, 107
Confucius, 19
Cook, Frederick A., 74
Cook, James, 50
Cooper, Martin, 100
Copernicus, Nicolaus, 6, 37, 45, 48
Cornwallis, Charles, 52
Cortés, Hernán, 39, 43
Crick, Francis, 92
Crimean War, 61
crops, 7, 9, 10, 12, 13, 27, 39, 59, 80, 92
Crusades, 25, 32–33
cuneiform, 14, 17
Curie, Marie, 69
Curie, Pierre, 69
Curiosity (spacecraft), 112

Daguerre, Louis, 59
Daimler, Gottlieb, 63
Dalton, John, 75
Darwin, Charles, 62
da Vinci, Leonardo, 37, 41
Davy, Humphry, 57
de Champlain, Samuel, 47
Declaration of Independence, 52, 97
Declaration of the Rights of Man, 54
de Coubertin, Pierre, 18
Deepwater Horizon, 114
de Klerk, F.W., 106
de Lesseps, Ferdinand, 65, 72, 73
della Francesca, Piero, 37
democracy, 16, 26, 105
Depression, Great, 83
diabetes, 81
Discovery (space shuttle), 106
DNA (deoxyribonucleic acid), 64, 79, 92

dodo, 49
Dolly, 109
Dust Bowl, 12
DVDs, 94

Eagle (lunar lander), 99
earthquakes, 16, 35, 104, 113, 115
East Germany, 95, 105
Edison, Thomas, 57, 67
education, 16, 29, 37, 38
Egypt, 15, 17, 65, 80, 81, 91, 114
Einstein, Albert, 21, 57, 72
electricity, 46, 56, 57, 60, 66, 67, 68, 69, 94
electric motor, 46, 51, 57
electromagnetism, 57
electrons, 75, 79
e-mail, 94
Empire State Building, 83
energy, 56, 63, 67, 72, 79, 89, 112
engines
    gasoline, 63
    internal combustion, 63, 68
    jet, 63
    steam, 7, 51, 53, 58, 63
England, 28, 30, 34, 36, 42, 46, 47, 51, 52, 53, 67, 76, 84, 86, 108. See also Britain
ENIAC, 88
environment, 96, 104, 114
Eric the Red, 30
Eriksson, Leif, 30, 31
Etruscans, 17, 18
euro, 108
European Union, 108
Everest, Mount, 92
evolution, 6, 62, 94
exploration, 6, 13, 23, 33, 40, 46, 50, 88, 93, 102
extinction, 49
Exxon Valdez, 104, 114
eyeglasses, 36
Eyjafjallajökull, 113

Facebook, 6, 110
factories, 28, 51, 53, 57, 58, 67
Faraday, Michael, 21, 57
farming, 7, 9, 11, 12, 13, 17, 27, 30, 39, 53, 59, 61, 64, 80
Farnsworth, Philo, 70
Ferdinand, Franz, 76
fertilizer, synthetic, 9, 59
Fessenden, Reginald, 70
fire, 6, 7
fishing, 13, 40
Fitzwalter, Robert, 34
Fleming, Alexander, 82
Fleming, Sandford, 67
flight, 41, 71
floods, 111, 113
flu. See influenza

food, 6, 7, 9, 10, 12, 17, 27, 39, 56, 59, 61, 63, 65, 73, 92, 115
Ford, Henry, 68
France, 36, 47, 49, 54, 65, 76, 86, 87, 108, 111
French Revolution, 52, 54
fuel, 9, 51, 63, 68

Gagarin, Yuri, 98, 99
Galilei, Galileo, 37, 48
Gandhi, Indira, 94
Gandhi, Mahatma, 84
gasoline, 12, 63, 68
Gates, Bill, 71
Gautama, Siddhartha. *See* Buddha
General Assembly, UN, 90, 91
generators, electric, 57
genes, 64, 92, 109
George III, King of England, 52
Germany, 76, 77, 85, 86, 87, 95, 105, 111
germs, 63
Gilbert, William, 46
glasses. *See* eyeglasses
global warming, 111, 113
Google+, 110
Gorbachev, Mikhail, 105
government, 10, 20, 26, 34, 44, 47
GPS (Global Positioning System), 21, 70
grains, 9
gravity, 49
Great Wall of China, 22
Greece, 16, 18, 20, 37
Guillet, James, 100
Gulf of Mexico, 39, 104, 114
gunpowder, 23, 32
guns, 27, 32, 39, 41, 42
Gutenberg, Johannes, 29, 37, 38

Haber, Fritz, 59
Hahn, Otto, 89
Hannibal, 24
Hardrada, Harald, 31
Harry Potter, 109
Hawking, Stephen, 48
heat waves, 111, 113
Henson, Matthew, 74
Herculaneum, 25
herding, 9, 11
heredity, 64
Herschel, John, 59
Hillary, Edmund, 92
Hippocrates, 16, 20
Hiroshima, 79, 87, 89
Hitler, Adolf, 85, 86, 87, 91
HIV (human immunodeficiency virus), 103
Holy Land, 32, 33
Homo sapiens, 6

horsepower, 11, 51
horses, 11, 12, 39, 43, 51, 58
Hubble Space Telescope, 49, 106
humans, early, 6, 7
Hundred Years' War, 36
hunting, 7, 9, 10, 11
Huygens, Christiaan, 35

ibn Abdullah, Muhammad, 28
ibn Hayyan, Jabir, 29
Ice Age, 10
Iceland, 113
India, 23, 44, 84
Industrial Revolution, 9, 28, 51, 53, 63
infections, 36, 63, 82, 103, 109
influenza, 55, 79
insulin, 81
integrated circuit, 94
internal combustion engine, 63, 68
International Space Station, 99
Internet, 65, 88, 93, 100–101, 107
Iran, 103
iron, 12, 17, 18, 61
Iron Age, 17
irrigation, 13, 27, 39
Irvine, Andrew, 92
Islam, 23, 28, 44, 103
Israel, 91, 100

Jamestown, 47
Japan, 79, 87, 89, 91, 104, 115
Jenner, Edward, 55, 63
Jericho, 10
Jerusalem, 32, 33
Jews, 78, 85, 87, 91
Joan of Arc, 36
John, King of England, 34
Johnson, Lyndon, 97
Jupiter, 27, 48, 93

Kai-shek, Chiang, 91
Kandinsky, Wassily, 74
Kennedy, John F., 97, 98
Kepler, Johannes, 48
Khan, Genghis, 33
Khan, Kublai, 33, 35
Khomeini, Ayatollah Ruhollah, 103
Khufu, Paroah of Egypt, 15
Kilby, Jack, 94
King, Martin Luther, Jr., 25, 42, 84, 97
Kline, Charley, 100
Koran, 28
Kumaratunga, Chandrika, 94

Laënnec, René, 56
Laika, 98, 99
Langerhans, Paul, 81
language, 8, 14, 17

laptops, 56, 88
lasers, 94
League of Nations, 77, 90
Leakey, Mary, 94
Lenin, Vladimir, 78
Lenoir, Étienne, 63
Licklider, Joseph Carl Robnett, 100
light, 7, 49, 57, 63, 67, 72, 94
  bulb, 67
locomotives, steam, 58
Long, Luz, 85
looms, 28, 53
Louis XVI, King of France, 54
Lucas, George, 102
Luna 9, 99

Magellan, Ferdinand, 43
Magna Carta, 34
magnetism, 21, 46, 57
Maiman, Theodore H., 94
malaria, 55, 72, 73
Mallory, George, 92
Manchester Small Scale Experimental Machine, 88
Mandela, Nelson, 106
manufacturing, 9, 53, 58, 68, 101
Marconi, Guglielmo, 57, 70
Mars, 27, 99, 102, 112
Mars (spacecraft), 99
Marx, Karl, 78
mathematics, 14, 15, 16, 21, 27, 33, 49
Mao Zedong, 91
Maya, 21
Maybach, Wilhelm, 63
medicine, 9, 16, 20, 33, 46, 69, 82
Mein Kampf, 85
Meir, Golda, 94
Meitner, Lise, 89
Mendel, Gregor, 64, 92
MESSENGER (spacecraft), 112
Michelangelo, 37, 41
microchips, 88, 90, 94, 101
microorganisms, 63, 100
microscopes, 48
microwave ovens, 70
Middle Ages, 16, 37
mining, 18, 51, 58
Minoans, 16
mold, 82
Mona Lisa, 41
Mondrian, Piet, 74
money, 108
Mongols, 23, 33, 44
Moon, 48, 71, 93, 98–99, 99
Morse code, 60, 70
Morse, Samuel, 60
motors, 12
  electric, 46, 51, 57
movies, 88, 100, 101, 102, 109

Mozart, Wolfgang Amadeus, 55
MP3s, 107
Mubarak, Hosni, 114
Mughal Empire, 44
Muhammad ibn Abdullah, 28
Murray, James, 59
Muslims, 28, 32, 33, 91
Mycenaeans, 16
Myspace, 110

Nagasaki, 79, 87, 89
NASA (National Aeronautics and Space Administration), 98, 99, 111
Nasser, Gamal, 65
National Association for the Advancement of Colored People, 42
National Socialist Party, 85
natural disasters, 100, 113, 115
natural selection, 62
navigation, 13, 21, 35, 46, 57, 93, 115
Nazi Party, 85, 86, 87, 91
networking, 100, 101, 110, 113
neutrons, 89
Newcomen, Thomas, 51
Newport, Christopher, 47
Newton, Isaac, 49
New World, 40, 43
New York City, 75, 83, 90, 110
New Zealand, 6, 68
Nicholas, Tsar, 76, 78
Niépce, Joseph Nicéphore, 59
Nightingale, Florence, 61
Nipkow, Paul, 70
Nobel prizes, 69, 97, 106
nomads, 11, 33
Norgay, Tenzing, 92
North Pole, 74
Northwest Passage, 50
nuclear
  bombs, 79, 89
  energy, 79, 89
  fission, 89
  power, 72, 89, 115
  reactors, 89, 104, 111
nucleus, 75, 79, 89
nylon, 73

Obama, Barack, 42, 113
oil, 57, 67, 104
  spills, 104, 114
Olmecs, 21, 49
Olympic Games, 18, 85
On the Magnet, 46
On the Origin of Species, 62
Ottoman Empire, 44, 61, 77
Owens, Jesse, 85

Pahlavi, Mohammad Reza, 103

painting, 8, 37, 41, 59, 69, 74
Palestine, 91
Panama Canal, 72–73
paper, 14, 23, 26, 38
papyrus, 14, 26
parchment, 26
Pasteur, Louis, 63
pasteurization, 63
peanuts, 80
Peary, Robert E., 74
penicillin, 82
Pentagon, 110
People's Republic of China, 91
Pericles, 16
Perskyi, Constantin, 70
pesticides, 96
Petrarch, Francesco, 37
philosophy, 16, 19
Phoenicians, 17
Phoenix (Mars lander), 112
photography, 59, 100
photons, 89
physics, 48, 49, 72, 79
Picasso, Pablo, 74
pictograms, 14
Picture with a Circle, 74
plague, 23, 36
Plaisted, Ralph, 74
planets, 27, 37, 45, 48, 49, 57, 59, 99, 106, 112
plastics, 9, 73, 100
  biodegradable, 73, 100
Plato, 16
plows, 9, 12, 14
Plymouth, Massachusetts, 47
Poland, 85, 86, 105
polio (poliomyelitis), 93
politics, 16, 24, 44
pollution, 10, 46, 53
Polo, Marco, 23, 33, 35
polonium, 69
Pompeii, 25
pottery, 7, 10, 12
power
  electricity, 57
  gas, 12
  gear, 35
  horsepower, 11, 51
  internal combustion engine, 63, 68
  nuclear, 72, 89, 104, 115
  solar, 106
  steam, 7, 12, 51, 53, 58
  turbine, 63
printing, 26, 29, 36, 37, 38
printing presses, 6, 26, 29, 37, 38
Protestant Reformation, 37
protons, 79
pumps, 13, 21, 51
pyramids, 15, 27
Pythagoras, 16

Qin Shi Huang, Emperor of China, 22
Qur'an, 28

radiation, 72, 89, 94, 104, 115
radio, 57, 70, 90, 93
radioactivity, 69, 79, 89, 104
radium, 69
railways, 58, 61
Raphael, 37
Raskob, John Jakob, 83
Red Cross, 25
refrigeration, 65
religion, 16, 25, 27, 28, 39, 40, 42, 43, 62, 103
Renaissance, 16, 37, 38
revolutions, 100
  Arab, 114
  American, 52
  French, 52, 54
  Industrial, 9, 28, 51, 53, 63
  Iranian, 103
  Russian, 77, 78
rice, 9
Roberts, Ed, 101
robots, 41, 82–83, 102
Romans, 17, 18, 24
Rome, 18, 24
Romeo and Juliet, 45
Röntgen, Wilhelm, 69
Rowling, J.K., 109
rubber, 49
Russia, 76–77, 78, 105
Russian Revolution, 77, 78
Russo-Japanese war, 78
Rutherford, Ernest, 75, 79, 89

Sahelanthropus, 6
sailing, 13, 21, 35, 46, 51, 57
Salk, Dr. Jonas, 93
salt, 84, 112
satellites, 35, 93, 98, 99
satyagraha, 84
schools, 14
scientific method, 29
SCORE (Signal Communication by Orbiting Relay Equipment), 93
scurvy, 43, 47, 50
Seven Years' War, 52
Shakespeare, William, 45
Sheppard, Kate, 68
ships, 13, 51, 61, 75
Shockley, William, 90
Silent Spring, 96
Silicon Age, 17
Silk Road, 23, 32, 33
Sistine Chapel, 41
skyscrapers, 61, 83
slavery, 27, 42, 47
smallpox, 27, 39, 55
smartphones, 66, 100
Smith, John, 47
social networking. *See* networking
Socrates, 16

South Africa, 106
Soviet Union. *See* Russia
space, 93, 106, 112
  probes, 93, 94, 102, 112
spacecraft, 71, 88, 98, 99, 102, 111, 112, 115
Spaniards, 27, 39, 43
spinning jennies, 28
spinning wheels, 26, 28, 53
Sputnik 1, 93, 98, 99
Stalin, Joseph, 86
Star Wars, 102
Starlite, 73
stars, 21, 48, 57, 106
steam, 7, 51
  engines, 51, 53, 58, 63
  power, 12, 53
  railways, 58
  ships, 13, 51
  trains, 51, 53, 58
steel, 61, 87
Stephenson, George, 58
stethoscopes, 56
Strassmann, Fritz, 89
Suez Canal, 65, 72
Suleiman the Magnificent, 44
Sumerians, 12, 14
Sun, 15, 21, 37, 45, 48, 49, 112
Syria, 16, 17, 91, 114

Taj Mahal, 44
Talbot, Henry Fox, 59
Tanaka Hisashige, 83
tape, adhesive, 73
taxes, 34, 39, 43, 44, 50, 52, 54, 84
technology, 45, 46, 53, 70, 88, 93, 100, 102, 115
telegraphs, 56, 60, 64–65, 66, 67, 81
telephones, 56, 60, 66, 90, 94. *See also* cell phones
telescopes, 48, 49, 99, 106, 112
television (TV), 46, 70, 90, 93
Televox, 82, 83
Tereshkova, Valentina, 99
terrorists, 110
thermometers, 48
Thomson, Joseph John, 75
Tiananmen Square, 105
time zones, 67
Titanic, 75
tools, 6, 7, 17, 27, 39, 53, 66, 107
trading, 9, 10, 12, 13, 14, 16, 17, 21, 23, 26, 27, 33, 35, 36, 42, 44, 47, 53, 107, 108
trains, 51, 53, 58, 108
transatlantic cable, 64–65
transistors, 88, 90, 94
transportation, 46, 65, 71, 73, 108

Travels of Marco Polo, The, 35
Truman, Harry, 89
tsunamis, 16, 25, 115
tuberculosis, 82
Tunisia, 114
turbines, 12, 63
Tutankhamen, Paroah of Egypt, 80–81
Twitter, 110

unions, 53
United Nations (UN), 87, 90, 91
United States of America, 42, 50, 52, 61, 65, 68, 73, 77, 80, 87, 89, 90, 97, 100, 110, 113, 114
uranium, 89
U.S.S.R. *See* Russia

vaccines, 55, 63, 93
vacuum tubes, 88, 90
Venera 7, 99
Venus, 27, 48, 99
Vesuvius, Mount, 25
videos, 96, 110
Vietnam War, 97
Viking (spacecraft), 99, 102, 112
Vikings, 30–31, 40
vinyl, 73
volcanoes, 25, 83, 113, 115
Volta, Alessandro, 56
von Linde, Carl, 65
voting, 20, 26
  women, 6, 68

Walesa, Lech, 105
Wall Street, 83
War of Independence, 52
Washington, George, 52
Watson, James, 92
Watson, Thomas, 66
Watt, James, 51
weather, 93, 113
websites, 101
Wensley, Roy, 82
wheels, 6, 12, 14, 68
Whites, 42, 80, 97, 106
World Trade Center, 83, 110
World War I, 44, 71, 76–77, 78, 80, 82, 85, 86, 90
World War II, 5, 6, 60, 77, 83, 85, 86–87, 89, 90, 91, 95, 108
World Wide Web, 6, 71, 88, 101, 107
Wright brothers, 71
writing, 14, 17, 27, 29, 37, 39

X-rays, 69

yellow fever, 72–73

Zedong, Mao, 91
zero, 15

**To Sarah, Robin, Scott, Beth, Ben, Bon, Hannah and Mia
and the spirit of adventure in them all — E.M.**

**To my wonderful writing partner, Liz, and in memory of
Aunt Helen, who made the world a better place — F.W.**

Acknowledgments

With warmest thanks to our wise editor, Val Wyatt. We couldn't have navigated the twists and turns of history without you!

Big thanks to Qin Leng for her detailed and delightful illustrations. Many thanks to designer Julia Naimska for making the words and images look great together. Thanks to copy editor Kathy Vanderlinden, for her skillful copy editing, and the staff at Kids Can Press.

Thanks to the many experts who helped answer our questions, including Jude Isabella.

Special thanks to Elena Zanetti and Michael Steeves for their help and support.

And with gratitude, as always, to Bill and Paul, who know just about everything!

Kids Can Press acknowledges the financial support of the Government of Ontario, through the Ontario Media Development Corporation's Ontario Book Initiative; the Ontario Arts Council; the Canada Council for the Arts; and the Government of Canada, through the CBF, for our publishing activity.

Published in Canada by
Kids Can Press Ltd.
25 Dockside Drive
Toronto, ON M5A 0B5

www.kidscanpress.com

The artwork in this book was rendered in pen and watercolor.
The text is set in Plantin and Futura Condensed.

Edited by Valerie Wyatt
Designed by Julia Naimska

This book is smyth sewn casebound.
Manufactured in Shenzhen, China, in 4/2013 by C & C Offset

CM 13 0 9 8 7 6 5 4 3 2 1

Published in the U.S. by
Kids Can Press Ltd.
2250 Military Road
Tonawanda, NY 14150

Library and Archives Canada Cataloguing in Publication

MacLeod, Elizabeth
A history of just about everything : 180 events, people and inventions that changed the world / written by Elizabeth MacLeod and Frieda Wishinsky ; illustrated by Qin Leng.

Includes index.
ISBN 978-1-55453-775-4

1. World history — Miscellanea — Juvenile literature.
2. Civilization — Juvenile literature. 3. Inventions — History — Juvenile literature. I. Wishinsky, Frieda
II. Leng, Qin   III. Title.

D20.M32 2013   j909   C2012-907765-8

Kids Can Press is a corus™ Entertainment company